Write a Use Case

Crafting Functional Requirements that Users Understand

with

Jonathan Reeve Price

Copyright

Copyright 2020 by Jonathan Reeve Price

Publisher: The Communication Circle

4704 Mi Cordelia Drive, NW

Albuquerque, NM 87120

http://www.webwritingthatworks.com

Published in the United States of America.

First Publication: 2020

ISBN: 978-0-9719954-5-1

All rights reserved

No part of this book shall be reproduced, stored in a retrieval system, or transmitted by any means, electronic, mechanical, photocopying, recording, or otherwise, without written permission from the publisher. No patent liability is assumed with respect to the use of the information contained herein. Although every precaution has been taken in the preparation of this book, the publisher and author assume no responsibility for errors or omissions. Nor is any liability assumed for damages resulting from the use of the information contained herein.

Trademarks

All terms mentioned in this book that are known to be trademarks or service marks have been appropriately capitalized. The Communication Circle and Jonathan Price cannot attest to the accuracy of this information. Use of a term in this book should not be regarded as affecting the validity of any trademark or service mark.

Warning and disclaimer

Every effort has been made to make this book as complete and as accurate as possible, but no warranty or fitness is implied. The information provided is on an "as is" basis. The author and the publisher shall have neither liability nor responsibility to any person or entity with respect to any loss or damages arising from the information contained in this book.

Quick: Is this book for you?

Yes, if you're a writer. Not a programmer. Not a suit.

Yes, if you want to craft requirements that are:

- Focused on user goals, tasks, and benefits
- Consistently organized, complete, and clear
- Understood and agreed-to by both stakeholders and developers
- Discussed extensively and collaboratively updated
- Used as a blueprint for code that meets or exceeds user expectations
- Transformed into test cases that measure your success

So this book helps you create a series of artifacts:

1. Descriptions of user needs, requests, and dreams
2. A list of features that might satisfy those demands
3. An overall vision for the proposed product
4. A set of requirement statements, if you must (deprecated)
5. A model diagramming all the possible use cases
6. Use cases that make sense to both stakeholders and developers
7. Test cases that prove that the code meets user goals
8. User stories, for smaller, more agile projects

What's next?

- Step-by-step instructions for creating the elements in each artifact
- Explanations of the *why* behind the *how* and the *what*
- Lots of yes-and-no examples
- A formal architecture that works with structured writing tools and content management systems
- Advice and tips based on the experiences of many writers working with development teams on large and small projects for consumer, corporate, and government customers
- Checklists for heuristic evaluations
- An index

Your role

As a writer, you help the project team discover the functional requirements—the ones that define what the product will do for the user. You act as a mediator between the stakeholders and the developers, helping them reach mutual understanding on what must be built.

The conversations that you host, moderate, and summarize can lead to real communication, increasing the likelihood that the product will meet and perhaps even exceed the expectations of the users. You are acting as an advocate for both groups--the users and your team—as you work together to clarify a vision of success.

Gathering requirements, then, demands empathy, imagination, and discipline. As you listen to what stakeholders are saying, you may need to probe the gaps, the silences where people seem to be hinting at something but not saying it. And as you hear the questions that developers are asking, you may need to clarify, summarizing in plain English, so stakeholders can respond with the relevant info.

Producing useful, clear, actionable requirements takes a lot of work. But you do not do this alone. You are at the center of a series of interviews and conversations, serving as a facilitator, scribe, questioner, supporter, speaker, listener, editor, tester, and moderator.

The short-term output is a series of documents, but the long-range goal is a product that does what users want. Seems simple, right?

But post mortems on dozens of failed projects show that the root causes are often badly written requirements—incomplete, inaccurate, ambiguous, irrelevant, or untestable. The solutions, developed by the folks who have been writing use cases and user stories over the last decade: a hundred little tactics, each designed to steer us away from some pothole, or bottomless pit. Those tips form the basis for this book.

You'll see the reasoning behind each element in the patterns that have become standard, the rationale for the structure, and the style that best describes each aspect of a use case or user story. You'll see what makes these requirements work.

There is no perfect way to write functional requirements. Your team will pick and choose among the elements in the patterns that I outline here. You'll add your own twists. And, in draft after draft, your stakeholders will beat on what you write, and you'll revise.

But the through line remains what the users want to do—their goals, their actions, the functions they hope your product will provide.

Our job, as writers, is to capture those dreams in prose.

Contents

Chapter 1. Overview 1

Chapter 2. Creating a vision 9

1. Identify stakeholder needs. 10
2. Analyze the problems. 14
3. Identify possible features. 18
4. Define minimal scope. 21
5. Position the product. 22
6. Sum up all this preliminary analysis in the Vision Document. 23
7. Set up a database to track these ideas. 26

Chapter 3. Writing requirement statements 27

Build a Requirement Statement. 29
Review the functional requirement statements together. 34

Chapter 4. Moving toward use cases 41

Start with a use-case model 42
1. Name the people who will use the system 43
2. Name the goal of the actor. 45
3. Put each goal—and nothing else—in an oval. 47
4. Connect the actor with one or more goals. 51

5. For each use case, identify any other systems that the system must talk to. 52

6. Organize the set of use cases in a way that makes sense to key stakeholders. 53

7. (Optional) Write a brief description of each use case. 55

8. Review the use-case model. 57

Chapter 5. Creating a use case 61

Example of a use case 62

What is a use case? 65

Extended example: A full use case 68

How is a use case different from a procedure? 72

The elements of the use case 75

1. Create a Name that reflects a goal or purpose of the primary actor. 79

2. Start tracking its Status. (Optional) 80

3. Edit the Brief Description. 81

4. List the Actors. 83

5. Insert a Requirements section only if circumstances warrant. (Optional) 85

6. State the Preconditions. 87

7. List all the Scenarios you will cover. 89

8. Build the Basic Flow. 92

9. Consider Subflows. 99

10. List Alternative Flows. 101

11. Identify Extension Points. (Optional) 104

12. Describe Post Conditions. 106

13. Add an Activity Diagram. (Optional) 108

Tips on writing use cases 112

Recognize that every group has its own style 114

Sample: From needs to a use case 118

Checklist for a use case 130

Chapter 6. Creating a test case 135

We write test cases for two audiences 135

Sample test case 137

Why do we test? 143

Five ways we test for quality 145

Finding users to test the software 152

Scheduling the user test sessions 153

Preparing to test usability 155

Preparing to test functionality 156

Write a complete test case for each scenario 158

Imagining your audiences 176

Running a test 179

Watch for usability problems as you test................................. 182

Write up defects and new requests 183

Chapter 7. About user stories.................................. 187

What is a user story? 187

Organizing user stories.. 193

User stories take on meaning as they go. 194

How do user stories compare with use cases?................... 196

Appendix: Nonfunctional requirements 201

Resources 205

Author's Note 206

Index 209

Chapter 1. Overview

A functional requirement is an artifact that you create to help people understand what a new product must do for the users.

- For developers, a functional requirement describes a **function** that must be created in the product.

- For stakeholders who are trying to imagine the proposed product, a functional requirement describes a **task** they want to accomplish, a series of interactions with the product that will lead a user to a meaningful goal.

So, as a writer, you have two main audiences. Two mindsets. Two different perspectives.

You are helping these different groups reach agreement on what must be built. That's a big challenge.

In the beginning of your project, your team faces questions like these:

- What do our stakeholders want?

- What do we, as developers, need to build?

- How can these two streams of wishes, needs, and dreams flow together as we create a new product?

Gathering requirements seems easy until you do it. This book outlines a process—a series of steps you can undertake to figure out what you must build into the new or improved system, bot, website, or utility. You'll find you are doing a lot of interviewing, empathizing, writing, sketching, negotiating, listening, intervening, bringing harmony to heated arguments, and moving on.

OK, so that's the bad news.

More bad news: Many projects have failed because they screwed up this process. In fact, a quarter to a third of all software development projects fail, and when a post mortem is done, we often find that bad requirements are to blame.

To avoid chaos, we create or adopt a formal process. Every organization, every project develops its own process for gathering requirements.

But there are common phases we all go through, similar activities that we all need to do, and similar artifacts that we produce, along the way.

Here's what we have to do:

1. Describe what stakeholders want, wish for, need. (If the project is relatively small, short-term, we might now go right to user stories, which serve to provoke discussions on agile projects, when we do not need the full detail provided by use cases).

2. Translate those felt needs into possible features of the new product.

3. Create some form of vision document describing the proposed project, justifying its budget and schedule, to persuade management to give the OK.

4. Focus on the requirements that describe what the users can actually do—the functional requirements.

    - Describe these functional requirements in statements, if the project is complex, and management insists. (Optional, but not optimal).

    - Build use cases that describe those functions in ways that make sense to both developers and users. (Large, and complex).

    - Or discuss user stories, building code in quick sprints, then trying it out on stakeholders, without documenting a lot of analysis up front. (Small, and agile).

5. Create test cases to make sure that the code we have built really meets the users' needs. (Required).

So there are three ways that we can gather requirements, each with its own process. In this book, I focus on use cases, but we'll see how they can grow out of requirement statements, and go well beyond them. And we'll take a quick look at user stories, for comparison. With all three approaches, the goal is to achieve an almost mythical state—user satisfaction.

You can think of the process as a series of questions and answers.

Q: What do stakeholders want, need, wish for?

> Artifact: A list of stakeholder needs.

Q: What do we add to the product to satisfy those needs?

> Artifact: A list of possible features.

Q: What is this project going to cost, and what are you going to build, in general terms?

> Artifact: Vision document.

Q: Can you break up those imaginary features into dozens of actual requirements, functions that the developers must build into the new product?

> Artifact: Requirement statements.

Q: To help users understand how all this functionality can help them reach their goals, could you describe the requirements in terms of step-by-step actions leading to those goals?

> Artifact: Use cases.

Q: Can we skip all the details, and get right to building some workable software that users can try out and give us feedback about right away?

> Artifact: User stories.

Q: How can we be sure that the code we have built really addresses the needs and expectations of stakeholders?

> Artifact: Test cases.

Moving beyond lists of requirement statements

Requirement statements are still with us, particularly in very large projects. Each statement describes one function that the system must provide. In some organizations, you may have to create a batch of these requirement statements, so this book shows how to do them right.

But the real audience, here, is the development team. Each statement describes one and only one function, in isolation, making it easy to build, but not so easy to understand as part of a task that a user might to do. Context is lacking.

When handed a list of hundreds of individual statements, most users' eyes glaze over, and their minds begin to fry. Many sign off on the list, hoping for the best.

Unfortunately, the best rarely arrives.

How come?

The statements go function by function, saying what the system will do. But the list does not group these statements into a series of coherent flows. The list does not map to the real tasks that users want to accomplish, or their goals. (One task may involve half a dozen of these new functions).

Users have a very hard time seeing how they would be able to use this function plus that function plus the other function as steps leading toward a goal of real value.

So users and their representatives may give the team a go-ahead without knowing, really, what they will get. When these folks see the final product, they are often disappointed, finding the new product difficult to use, irrelevant to their work, out of date before release, or just plain unfriendly.

To avoid these risks, we turn to use cases.

What's a use case?

A use case describes one task that people will be able to do when they use the product that your team is about to develop or improve.

You write a use case for two audiences: the stakeholders and the developers.

- For stakeholders, your use case describes a goal that means something to their users, and the steps that the users will take, using the new product, to get to that goal.

- For developers, your use case describes one or more functions that must be built into the new system, to allow the users to accomplish that task.

For both audiences, then, the use case acts as a contract. The use case says what MUST be developed. Like a suitcase, it contains all the functional requirements for a particular task, organized in steps that make sense to both users and developers, so they can reach a real agreement, up front, before coding starts.

Why bother?

We create use cases to reduce or eliminate some of the risks that can plague us when gathering requirements.

- **Navel-gazing**: The developers come up with all the requirements, assuming that they know just what users want, without talking to them.

- **Ambiguity**: The users understand the statements one way, but the developers interpret the language differently, producing functions that the users dislike.

- **Sprawl**: So many tangled and overlapping requirements that no one—the stakeholders or the developers—can really see how everything fits together to let a user get a particular task done. Result: Crucial requirements get overlooked, left out, built in isolation.

- **Decay**: The stakeholders' lives keep changing, but the requirements do not change with them.

- **Unresponsiveness**: The requirements that the developers collect do not really reflect what stakeholders want or need. Result: The product turns out to be irrelevant, or counter-productive.

- **Scope creep**: No one resists the constant onrush of demands from stakeholders, resulting in too many patches, twists, and turns, complicating the functionality, and leading to a confusing user interface.

- **Lack of traceability**: As requirements change, the team has no way of going back to figure out what the real user needs might have been, or what folks originally requested, so the functions wander off course, making the product weak, or useless.

So as we build a use case, it is:

- **Discussed**: The subject of repeated conversations between users and developers, as they consider what each step means, and what options may arise.

- **Understood**: A way to make sure that both stakeholders and developers understand and agree on what should be built.

- **Focused**: A small set of requirements that can be talked about, planned for, understood as a whole, isolated from other requirements.

- **Adaptable**: Always open to updating, discussion, revision, in an iterative process.

- **Traceable**: You can go back to find what user needs prompted the use case, what revisions have been made to the use case, what code is related to the use case, and what test cases and results stem from the use case. That's very helpful for updating and revising later.

How do we get from user needs to use cases?

We follow a formal process. Because requirements can determine the success or failure of the final product, driving the satisfaction of the users, generations of project teams have evolved standard guidelines, and well-thought-out processes for creating all these artifacts.

In this book, we follow a rather elaborate process that was developed by some of the leading object-oriented programmers and refined by project managers—the Rational Unified Process, known colloquially as "RUP."

But there are no sacred standards for gathering requirements. Most organizations have their own set of artifacts, their own processes.

So the elements that you create may not be the same as the ones I describe here. Your audiences may need more or less, your project may be bigger or smaller, your team may be more or less self-aware, empathetic, or pig-headed.

At first, you may find all the guidelines a bit overwhelming—there are so many. But for each one, remember that it was only invented to prevent us falling into some ditch that many people before us tumbled into. For each suggestion, then, imagine what could go wrong if you did not follow it, or adapt it to your own situation.

If you are new to product development, you may struggle to understand the process, and within that, the documents that mark its milestones. But on the job, the process is not so intimidating. You work as part of a team. You help the developers understand the users, and you help the users understand what they are having built. In this way, you are at the center of a series of conversations. You are not inventing the product; you are helping it grow.

You get a lot out of participating in this activity.

- Learning what users really want, what they are afraid of, what they get angry about

- Understanding the life or work situation in which users are likely to be using the product

- Participating in debates about the way a feature should work, so you get to speak up for the user ("If we ourselves don't understand how this function is going to work, how will a user figure it out?")

- Helping developers keep on track, by pointing out the times when they are veering away from the original requirements

- Acting as a spokesperson for the user whenever you sense inconsistency, confusion, or baffling sequences of arbitrary actions.

- Establishing close ties with the programmers, marketing folks, quality control team, user interface experts, and support teams—making sure that all their views are heard, and incorporated into the documents as you write them

- Communicating all the information that your team develops, publishing it for internal use by other groups, such as marketing, manufacturing, sales, support—all the people who traditionally do NOT get much advance notice of new products

- Establishing yourself as an important part of a process that lies at the core of the business—creating products that people really need, maybe even products they will love.

You do not create all this content by yourself. You interview stakeholders, you talk to ordinary users, you talk to developers.

You go to meetings where developers talk to representatives of the users—and you record the agreements. You do not invent the requirements. You get them down as accurately as you can.

In fact, one way that you contribute to the success of the project is that you help both groups—users and developers—clarify their language, reach a real mutual understanding. Your text records those agreements.

And in the next meeting, your document serves as the basis for more conversation. You record more changes. You point out inconsistencies, disagreements, unexplored possibilities. You help everyone think.

But by yourself you do not have to come up with the requirements. You make it possible for the team to gather them, record them, interrogate them, change them, and, eventually, test them, and publish the resulting product. You are at the center of the conversation, sympathetic to the questions raised by developers, but also eager to help the users get the product that they need.

Write a Use Case

Chapter 2. Creating a vision

Early in a project, the team needs your help in figuring out what kind of product to build. They may be hearing conflicting stories from

- Users
- The marketing group
- The sales group
- The support team.

And as developers, they have their own pet projects they would like to explore, neat new technical feats that may or may not have value for the user.

How can the team produce a coherent picture of the new product?

You can help the team develop a vision of the product, as you work toward a document that marketing likes to call, cue the violins, *The Vision Document*.

As you work with the team to develop this description of the proposed product, so that upper management can authorize the budget, you go through these steps:

1. Identify stakeholder needs.
2. Analyze the problems.
3. Identify possible features.
4. Define minimal scope.
5. Create a product positioning statement.
6. Sum up all this preliminary analysis in the Vision Document.
7. Set up a database to track these ideas.

1. Identify stakeholder needs.

What's a stakeholder need?

A **need** is a longing, a wish, a dream. You may discover these needs in interviews with stakeholders. You may get specific requests from some folks. You may pore over bug reports, and spot needs in the most common questions asked of the support teams. You are recording the users' pains, their problems, their longed-for opportunities—whatever might motivate them to pay for your team to develop a new or improved system.

Formally, a **need** is an expression of the stakeholder's desired state in the *subject domain*, or in the software (known as the *solution space*).

Examples of stakeholder needs:

- Administrators need to spend less time handling each registration.
- Professors need immediate access to student grades.
- We have got to have a single work control process, across all groups.

A need is not a requirement. It does not have enough detail to show developers how the function should work; it cannot be tested, measured, verified. It remains vague, emotional, and poorly defined. But it points to what you should build.

First find the stakeholders—the ultimate sources of requirements.

These are all the people who are affected by the problem, not just the immediate users.

Sponsors:

- Business manager
- Finance chief
- Shareholder
- Champion of the project
- Seller
- Marketer
- Steering committee members
- Investors

Authorities:

- Laws, rules, policies
- Standards organizations
- Organizational governance teams
- Domain experts
- Technology experts

Affected personnel:

- As you begin to get a glimpse of the solution, include anyone who would be affected by that.
- Indirect stakeholders such as a help desk manager, who has to support the solution, or an installation team, who have to mount the software.

A **stakeholder**, then, is anyone who is materially affected by the outcome of the system or the project producing the system.

But you do not have to consult every stakeholder group.

Focus on the ones who have the most to lose if the problems are not solved, or the opportunities are lost.

Describe your stakeholders.

In the Vision document that you are developing, you need to give management a good picture of the stakeholders, and their problems or challenges.

For each stakeholder group, provide information such as:

- Name of that group
- Representative for that group
- Description
- Background and experience
- Responsibilities
- Criteria they will use to judge whether the project is a success
- Involvement (how they will be involved in using the product)
- Deliverables (what they will provide, such as review comments)
- Comments or concerns

Cast a wide net.

Collect information from stakeholders.

- Initial requests
- Bug reports
- Change requests
- User forum postings
- Calls to support
- Business models, constraints

Learn the business domain through…

- Site visits
- Meeting with domain experts
- Attending workshops and conferences
- Studying competitive analysis
- Policies and procedures
- Laws and regulations

Keep the discussion going. You may have to discuss your descriptions of the stakeholders with your team, and then submit these descriptions to the stakeholders themselves, to get cooperation and agreement.

Problems you may encounter:

- Stakeholders have a pre-conceived idea of a solution.
- Nobody knows what they really want.
- Stakeholders are inarticulate, ambiguous, confusing.
- Analysts think they know best.
- Everyone has a limited point of view.

To resolve issues, interact with stakeholders in whatever ways you can:

- Review any initial requests for help.
- Hold a requirements workshop.
- Do one-on-one interviews.

- Hand out surveys or questionnaires.
- Do role playing.
- Build prototypes and ask if they meet the need.
- Create storyboards and try out on the stakeholders.

Treasure any requests that come directly from the stakeholders, but distinguish between:

- What the application should do
- What people should do
- Other issues and assumptions

Interview as many people as possible, to learn what they mean by the requests.

- Probe to see if these requests express real needs…or if they have jumped right to their idea of a solution (a set of features).
- You need to figure out the need behind the requested feature, so you can decide whether that feature is really the way to meet the need.
- If presented with a proposed feature, ask why.

Example of a stakeholder requesting a feature:

Request: "I want the defect tracking system to provide a full project status trending report."

Question: "Why?"

Actual need: "I need to see how long it is taking us to resolve defects each month, to track trends."

Ideal: Create a separate document or database to store all Stakeholder Requests so the team can look these up during development.

- Collect all requests from all sources.
- Include emails, interview notes, napkin ideas, white board scans.
- Make this data available to the team as they define features and then software requirements.

2. Analyze the problems.

Analyze stakeholder definitions of the problems they face.

In interviews and team discussions, explore the gap between what stakeholders perceive is the current reality and what they would like.

Why?

- Their perception may be wrong. (The feature may already exist, for example.)
- Their dream may be too grandiose. (The feature may cost too much, take too much time to build.)
- If there is a real gap between current reality and their desire, you can begin to visualize the solution together.

To avoid rework, make sure your team is working on the right problems.

Explore the root causes of the problems.

You want to avoid delivering a solution only to hear, "But that doesn't solve my real problem."

The root cause may be thought of as the real problem.

Identify possible causes and explore them.

- You may discover that two of the causes are actually the same ones.
- You may discover that some "causes" are totally irrelevant.
- You may discover problems hiding within other problems.

Analyzing the Perceived Problem: Customers Closing Accounts

Bank app does not display details on transactions

Bank app takes one or two seconds to bring up account.

Bank app cannot scan checks for deposit

Root causes

Bank site downtime exceeds 20hrs/month

Bank app takes five seconds to send two-factor code.

Make sure you understand the business or social context.

- Is there a cultural or process problem?
- Are there overlapping domains, turfs?
- Are there stakeholders who have an interest in maintaining the status quo?
- Are some stakeholders in conflict with others?

If necessary, create a Business Model, answering questions such as:

- How does the business operate now?
- What are the existing processes?
- Is the business going to change its processes, when it begins to use this new tool?
- What exactly will you be automating?

Components of the Business Model:

- Business processes
- Products
- Events
- Organizational structure
- Roles and responsibilities

Goals of a Business Model

- Understand the full context for the current problems
- Ensure that all stakeholders have the same understanding of the organization and its business
- Provide the basis for eliciting requirements

Grow your glossary as you go.

- Define terms used in the project, particularly ones that seem to provoke discussion in meetings.
- Keep expanding the glossary and refining it.
- Indicate preferred terms and mention the deprecated terms.

- Use these terms consistently in all your documentation.

If the stakeholders and developers are not in full agreement on the way the business works, create a Domain Model.

A **Domain Model** offers a visual model of key business objects.

When do you need a Domain Model?

> When you find that people are discussing what each object really is, and what the nature of the relationships are.

Make sure all these ideas are defined in the **glossary**.

Indicate relationships, with cardinality.

Example:

> One trading account can have an unlimited number of transactions associated with it.
>
> Each transaction is associated with one, and only one account.
>
> One customer has one or more accounts.

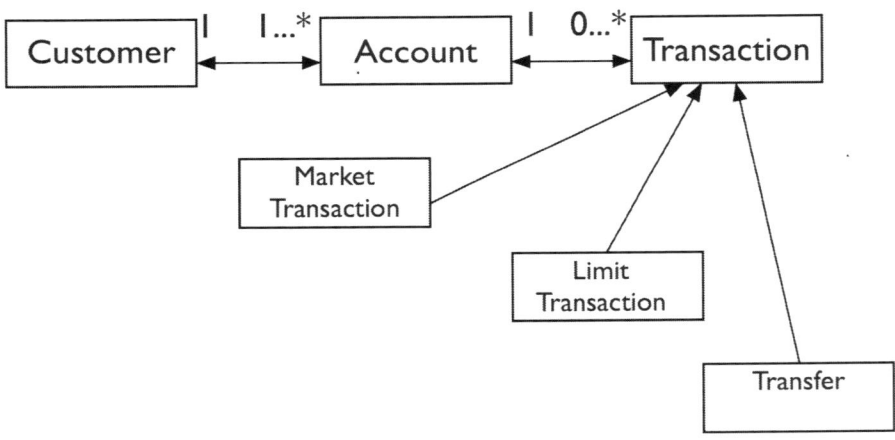

Identify possible solutions.

Check to make sure the proposed product actually addresses the root causes.

Focus on the most important root causes.

- The Pareto Principle (20% of the effort yields 80% of the benefit) applies. (A small number of contributing causes have a major impact; so those are the ones you should focus on.)

- Rank the contributing causes in the order of magnitude: How much does each contribute to the problem?
- If 80% of the problem is caused by two top contributors, focus on them.

Identify the best solution.

- What best solves the root causes?
- What best achieves the business's goals?

The details of the solution may become **features**.

3. Identify possible features.

A feature is an externally observable service—something that the new system should do.

- It **fulfills** a stakeholder request, **satisfies** a stakeholder need, **solves** a user problem.
- The description of the feature takes the system perspective.
    (Later you will create requirements from a user's perspective, in use cases.)
- The feature has some effect that should be observable by users, operators, or another system.

Examples:

> The ATM will allow a customer to transfer funds between accounts.
>
> The system will provide one location where a student may register for courses.

Brainstorm to generate ideas of features to address the needs, or solve the problems.

Write potential features on stickies.

- Let your imagination go.
- Do not criticize or debate.

Examples:

- The system must work with our existing access control system.
- There must be some kind of security.
- Maybe there should be different categories of users, like managers and workers.
- If I am already in the company system, I should be allowed into the new app, without having to enter my login and password a second time.
- The system should automate the flow of work, including, approval, notification, and escalation of transactions through the lifecycle of the corrective action.

2. Creating a vision

Classify the stickies, without discussion.

- Get people to organize the stickies.
- You are pulling together affinity groups.
- It's OK to add a few stickies at this time.

Name that feature.

- The facilitator reads a group of stickies, and asks the group to name that feature.
- You may get rid of some stickies, split groups.
- Goal: End up with 12-17 groups.

Boil the ideas down, prune, and organize.

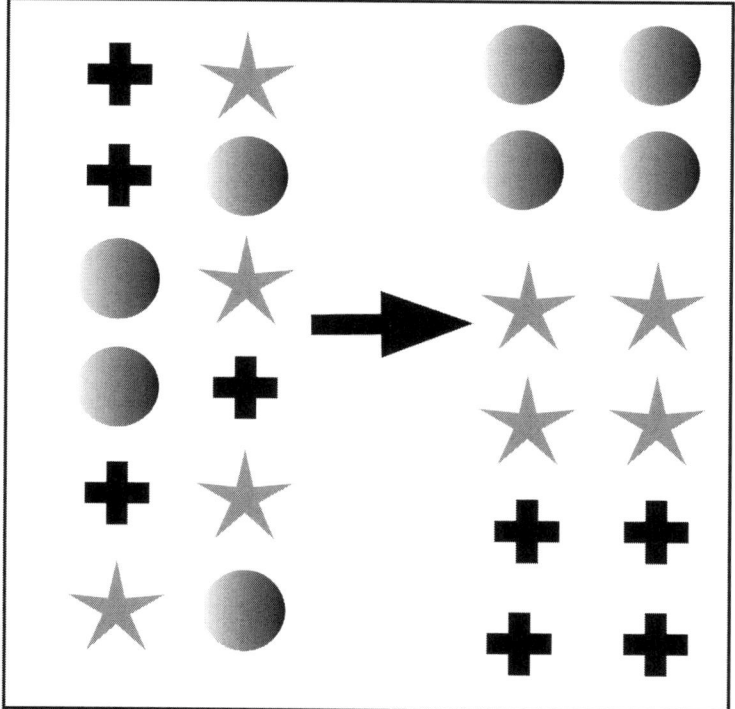

Prioritize the features.

- Which are key?
- Give people a limited number of votes, and see how they parcel those out.

Create the baseline set of features.

> The **baseline** is the set of features that have been agreed upon for development. The baseline features can only be changed through some formal procedure.

(Optional) Put a list of the features, along with attributes, in an appendix at the end of the Vision Document. Attributes:

- Rationale
- Priority
- Description
- Context

Why aren't features good enough, as requirements?

- They are just shorthand for what the system must do. They sound like marketing points.
- Many features are too vague to use when designing, developing, or testing the system. Others are too specific to make into a "must," such as the color of a button that may or may not appear in the final product.
- Stakeholders often think in terms of systems they already know, "solving" problems with "features" that are not optimal.
- In making requests, stakeholders rarely think through the implications of different features working together.
- One feature may involve half a dozen different functions in the software, and those functions have yet to be defined.
- Features rarely mention errors, exceptions, or problems.

So a feature is not a requirement.

For now you have a baseline set of features. Later, when your Vision document is approved, and you have a budget and schedule, you will work with the development team and representatives of the users to come up with the actual requirements.

4. Define minimal scope.

Clarify the system's boundaries, to avoid scope creep.

- Where does this system end? Where do other systems begin?
- Where does the data live?
- Where does data go? (To other systems, for instance, or a reporting tool).
- Who uses the system? (Who enters the data? Who can read the data? Who actually has access to the system?)
- To what extent will the functionality of this new system overlap, replace, or just plain duplicate what exists now?
- Is the client software part of the system, or is it just another actor, interacting with the system?

Define what is in scope, and what is out.

- You are trying to avoid confusion later, when users assume that you are going to do *xyz*, but you intend to do only *x*.
- You are negotiating a minimum set of features, and declaring everything else out of scope—for now.
- You are resisting stakeholder appeals for a total solution all at once.

5. Position the product.

A Product Position statement describes the whole product, as it will be when all features have been implemented. You are communicating the intent and the importance of the product, but you must do so in a paragraph or two. Not pages and pages.

Ask yourself: What makes this product unique, valuable, unusual, better than the existing product, or a competitor?

Use the problem statement as a starting point.

State the unique selling proposition for the product in the marketplace. Sell the idea in a few words.

The Product Position statement answers questions such as:

- Who is it for?
- What need does it address?
- What is the product category?
- What are the key benefits, the compelling reason to buy it?
- What are the competing products?
- How is this product unique, different?

6. Sum up all this preliminary analysis in the Vision Document.

You pull together what you have learned as you gather information about the proposed product and its stakeholders, putting all that in one document that argues for the product. You write to persuade all stakeholders that you should proceed to develop the product.

The Vision Document:

- Ensures that everyone is working from the same page.
- Circulates to management, marketing, project team, customer representatives, eliciting stakeholder feedback.
- Establishes the scope and priority of high-level stakeholder requests and features.
- Describes the what, and the why of the product.
- Forms the basis of conversations with upper management, soliciting funds and resources to develop the product.
- Acts as a contract (formal or informal).

Outline of the Vision Document

Introduction

Positioning the Product

> How is the new system going to be different from an earlier version? Competitive products?
>
> What is the marketing position statement?

Stakeholders and Users

> Who are they?
>
> What is their business situation?
>
> What are their needs?
>
> (Optional) Domain Model, or description of the nature of the business

Problem Definition

> Even if you are defining a set of interrelated problems or challenges, keep each one short.

Model for a problem definition:

> The problem of *x*
>
> Affects *y* (who).
>
> The result is *z*.
>
> A successful solution would be *abc*.

Product Overview

> What's it going to do?
>
> What are you going to call it?
>
> What are the main benefits?

Product Features (list with descriptions of each feature)

Priorities (among Features)

> Which ones are most important?
>
> Which involve the most risk?
>
> Which should be developed first?

Scope

> What will the system cover?
>
> What is out of scope?

Constraints

> These may look small at first, but they have a big impact.
>
> Some of these constraints affect the political decisions, such as budget, schedule, and resources.
>
> Types of constraints:
>
>> Environmental
>>
>> Political
>>
>> Financial
>>
>> Technical (platform, data standards, tools)
>>
>> Feasibility

Other Aspects of the Product

> These are informal descriptions of what will probably become non-functional or supplementary requirements.

2. Creating a vision

Documentation Vision (your preliminary plan)

Appendix: Features with Attributes

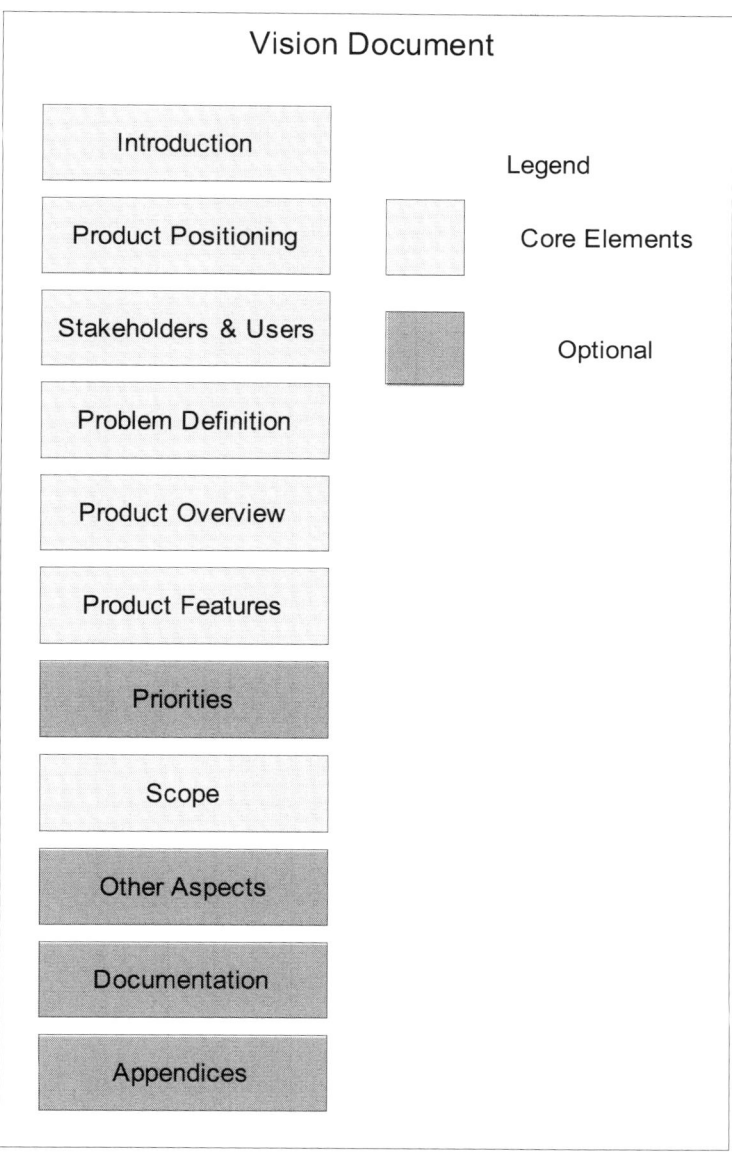

7. Set up a database to track these ideas.
Throughout this process, trace these objects.

We need to be able to trace back from an implemented requirement to the original need, and forward from one need to the many features that may have spawned. Why?

- Management uses the database to confirm that all needs have been met; all features provided; all requirements satisfied; all test cases passed.
- If the customer is unhappy, we need to be able to say, here is why we built it that way, just as you asked.
- When we decide to make a change to a feature, we want to know: why did we put this in here in the first place? What else does it affect?
- When some other team has to maintain the product, they may ask: What were you thinking? Why did you build it this way? And if we tinker with this little feature over here, what else might be affected?

For large, complex projects (over a few million dollars in budget), we use a database to trace every:

- Customer need
- Requested feature
- Requirement (usually in the form of use cases)
- Test case
- Designed object that corresponds to the use cases
- Procedure that describe how the user can perform the actions described in the use cases

This database shows impacts forward and back:

- One need leads to one or more features.
- One feature leads to one or more requirements.
- One requirement leads to one or more test cases.
- One test case points to one or more procedures in the user guide.
  Therefore, changing one little requirement may impact several test cases and multiple procedures, down the line.

Chapter 3. Writing requirement statements

When your Vision is approved, you work with the team to create specific requirements.

A requirement is a description of a condition or capability to which the system **must** conform.

- It may be derived directly from what users say they need, or from features they agree should be in the system.
- It may also be derived from some formally imposed authority, such as a contract or a standard.

A requirement specifies what the system **must** do, rather than how the system does it.

In meetings, we create different kinds of **requirements**—for example, functional requirements, non-functional requirements, and design constraints.

- A **functional requirement** specifies how the solution will interact with the outside world, including, most importantly, users. It does not say how the system does that.

    Example:

    > Functional: When the student chooses to Register, the system displays the list of available courses.

    Functional requirements may appear as **statements** or **use cases** or both. (More about that later).

- A **non-functional requirement** is a requirement that does not deal with the functions that a user gets to touch. It is "other." These requirements define specs for issues such as general usability, overall reliability, performance metrics, and supportability. (Another name for this kind of requirement: *supplementary*).

    Example:

    > Non-Functional: The system shall be available 99% of 24/7 (3.65 days of downtime per year).

    Non-functional requirements appear as **statements**.

- A **design constraint** is a limitation on the way the system is designed, built, or deployed.

Examples of design constraints:

> The system must operate on the IBM Z® System.
>
> The team must use the Eclipse Platform.

Design constraints usually appear as **statements**.

In organizations that still follow traditional methods, developers describe each requirement in one statement—one sentence.

A set of requirement statements for a simple system, then, can run to forty or fifty statements. For a moderately complex program, you may have a list of several hundred statements.

Users care most about functional requirements, though, because these describe the functions that will directly support their tasks, their goals. The users or their representatives come into meetings with developers to hash out the functional requirements, whether those are codified as statements or step-by-step use cases.

To make sure that your functional requirements are easy for users to understand, yet clear enough for developers to build on, you often have to step into the discussion to clarify language.

Examples:

- Two developers are using the same term to mean two different things.
- Three developers are using three different terms when they all mean the same thing.
- Stakeholders have come up with duplicate requirements in slightly different language.
- People are drafting requirements in vague, confusing, or deliberately opaque language.

As the writer, then, you walk a tightrope, balancing between developer talk, and ordinary words that stakeholders can understand. Your team may be old-fashioned, and demand that you describe functional requirements as a series of statements, or they may tilt toward use cases, as more user friendly…and in rare cases, a team may use both approaches.

In this section, then, we explore how to write functional requirement statements. In the next section, we turn to use cases.

Build a Requirement Statement

Give each statement an identifying number.

Tip: Never change that number.

Why?

Even if you edit the statement five times, you should keep the identifying number so that people can keep track of the way that statement has changed. Also, the database that stores your requirements can use that ID to trace the different versions; that's useful if you need to revert to an earlier draft, or figure out how that requirement has changed over time.

How?

Every group has its own numbering system. Often there is a prefix such as FR for Functional Requirement, followed by a number: FR32.

If your team decides to eliminate a requirement, just style it with strikethrough text, but preserve the original number, and save the statement in your database with notes about the rationale for dropping it.

Write one sentence describing what the system must do.

Keep it simple.

One sentence, one requirement.

Examples:

The system must store a record of each transaction.

The system must authenticate the user's identity before giving the user access to the public forum.

For each requirement, create a separate statement.

Not good:

FR33: The system must verify that any data entered into the Quantity field is a whole number, and that the number is between 1 and 12, and if the data is not a number, or if the data is a number other than 1, 2, 3, 4, 5, 6, 7, 8, 9,10, 11, or 12, then the system must display an alert requesting that the user insert a number between 1 and 12. The system must verify all data entered into fields on the Request form upon submission.

Better:

> FR33: The system must verify that any data entered in the Quantity field is a whole number from 1 to 12.
>
> FR34: If verification indicates that non-numeric data has been entered into the Quantity field, the system must display an alert requesting a number from 1 to 12.
>
> FR35: When verification indicates that a number outside the range of 1 to 12 has been entered, the system must display an alert requesting a number from 1 to 12.
>
> FR36: The system must verify all the fields on the Request form on submission.

Tip: When you find people asking for more than one requirement within a single sentence, or worse, adding several sentences, be on guard: You are edging toward describing multiple requirements.

Why not cram several requirements into one statement?

Having each requirement in its own statement, rather than several all at once, makes each requirement easier to analyze and discuss.

Yes, one requirement may lead to another (as when you say that the system will have a list of images, and later you say that the list will include the file size of each image). But when you are talking about the requirements, people can focus more cleanly on each individual requirement when it is isolated from others.

Eventually, your team will build the functionality and test it. If you have to test three different requirements, and they all have to be met at once, you may have to set up a lot more test conditions (if a and b but not c; if b and c but not a; and so on).

Testing for success is much easier when there is only one criterion for success, not three or four.

As an auxiliary verb, use either *must* or *shall*. Not *should*, *may*, or *will*.

Not good:

> The system will provide a way to switch between inches and pixels as units of measure.

Better:

> The system must provide a way to switch between inches and pixels as units of measure.

Not good:

> The system provides an image inspector that reports the file size.

Better:

> The system must provide an image inspector that reports the file size.

Tip: Use the same verb—either *must* or *shall*—**throughout** your set of requirements, to avoid debates about the difference between them.

Describe what the system must do, not what the user must do.

Not good:

> The user must change the CAW password once a month.

Better:

> The system must require that users change their passwords once a month.

Not good:

> The user has the ability to enter the ZIP code manually by typing.

Better:

> The system must offer a way to type in the ZIP code.

Make the requirement measurable.

In the future, developers will build this function. We need to know how to test that functionality to make sure that we have met the requirement. So we have to include measures of success, or targets that we can objectively check.

Not good:

> The system must export an image to a bitmap file format.

Better:

> The system must export an image to a jpg file format.

Not good:

> When the user chooses to quit, an alert offering to save the current file must appear within a few seconds.

Better:

> When the user chooses to quit, an alert offering to save the current file must appear within one second.

Do not describe the business.

Avoid describing how the stakeholders perform their tasks now.

Avoid setting policy for the users.

Do not describe the actual interface, or the algorithms in the code—leave that work for the designers to do later.

Not good:

> The Window menu must provide an option for Zoom.

Better:

> The system must provide a way to zoom the image.

Edit the language to eliminate possible misinterpretations.

Avoid the normal.

Replace or delete adverbs like *usually*, *generally*, *often*, *normally*, or *typically*. Persuade the team to come up with an objective measurement, or drop the term.

Use actual measures instead of vague adjectives.

Pin the stakeholders down. What do they mean when they describe something in contrasting statuses like the following?

- Good vs bad
- Strong vs weak
- High vs low
- Effective vs ineffective
- Fast vs slow

What do they mean by adjectives implying value judgments?

- Significant
- Adequate
- Appropriate
- Relevant

Avoid giving permission.

Steer clear of words such as: *may, can, optionally, might, should, could, perhaps, probably.*

Not good: The system may provide a circular selection tool.

Better: The system must provide a circular selection tool.

Avoid fantasy.

Not good: The system must achieve 100% accuracy in optical character recognition.

Better: The system must achieve 98% accuracy in optical character recognition, as measured by the THT test.

Offer ways of objectively measuring success.

Not good: The system must respond quickly to an incoming ping.

Better: The system must respond to an incoming ping within one second.

State the positive version.

There are a lot of parts of *no* that people do **not** understand.

Not good: The system must not drop a user without warning, advising the user that work may be lost if not saved.

Better: Before dropping a user, the system must display a warning, advising the user to save work.

If you must use jargon, define it in the glossary.

You may use the term several times in the requirements, so define it once in the glossary (not in the set of requirements).

Watch those referents.

Don't use a pronoun, adverb, or adjective to refer back to something you mentioned in an earlier requirement. Restate the term.

- What is *it*?
- Who are **they**?
- What is **that**?
- Where is **above**?

Use only one term for the same thing, throughout.

Is a **member** also a **beneficiary**, and are they both **subscribers**?

Store each requirement statement in a database.

Create a minimal set of fields to describe a statement, but only create fields that will help you or the developers do real work. Here are some that might be useful. (But remember, for every field that you create, you have to enter a value for each statement that you write).

- Unique identifier (Requirement #32)
- Source, if known (Who asked for this?)
- Priority (How important is it?)
- Type of requirement (For example, functional).
- Date of each change
- Rationale or discussion of changes
- Pointer to user needs related to this statement
- Pointer to feature description related to this statement
- Pointer to related test case
- Revision history

Review the functional requirement statements together.

In a traditional development environment, you meet repeatedly with the developers and people representing the users, to go over every statement, several times.

Goals:

- Get agreement from customers and other stakeholders on what the system must do.
- Provide developers with an understanding of the requirements.
- Delimit the system, defining its boundaries.
- Lay the basis for planning the technical aspects of the product.
- Provide the basis for estimating cost and time.

As a team, put each requirement statement under the microscope.

A requirement should be...

Correct

Tests:
- Is it a true statement of what the system must do?
- Is it really something the system must do?
- Do stakeholders or subject matter experts confirm that this requirement is correct?

Consistent

Tests:
- Does this requirement conflict with any other requirements?
- Does it conflict with any non-functional requirements or supplementary specs?
- Are the terms the same ones used in other requirement statements, and the glossary?

Unambiguous

Test:
- Is this requirement subject to one and only one interpretation?
- Do all stakeholders agree on that interpretation?
- Has every word been discussed, and agreed upon?

Verifiable

Tests:
- Can this requirement be tested? (How can you tell if this requirement has really been met?)
- Is there a feasible and cost-effective process that could test to see if this requirement has been implemented?

Unique

Test:

- Is there another requirement that says the same thing, or almost the same thing? (If so, delete one).

Ranked for Priority

Test:

- Is this requirement tagged with an indication of its importance or stability?

As a whole, a set of functional requirement statements should be:

Complete

Tests:

- Does it describe all the significant requirements of concern to the stakeholders?
- Have you included values for all the attributes for each requirement?
- Have you identified the ranges of input values expected in all possible scenarios?
- Have you included responses to both valid and invalid input values?
- Are all terms defined in a glossary?

Modifiable

Tests:

- Can you change the requirements easily, completely, and consistently without losing the style and structure of individual requirements?
- If there are overlapping requirements, are they cross-referenced?

Traceable

In your database, you should be able to trace back from each functional requirement to at least one relevant feature and from the feature back to at least one original stakeholder need.

- If a requirement does not directly fulfil a stakeholder need, you could be looking at scope creep.
- If a stakeholder need does not point forward to at least one particular requirement, you have forgotten to create at least one requirement.

Traceability proves completeness.

But we will also need traceability later as we modify or expand our requirements, to answer questions like these:

- If we change this particular requirement, will we still be fulfilling the original requests? Will the revised requirement reflect the feature we started with?
- If we change this requirement, what impact will that have on the project as a whole, and other components?
- If some test fails, are there some requirements that we have not satisfied?
- Is a proposed new requirement really within scope?
- Have we implemented everything that was in the original set of requirements?

Tests:

- Does each requirement have a unique identifier?
- Is every requirement distinguishable from the others?
- Is the origin of the requirement stated in the database record for the requirement?
- Does the database record for the requirement explicitly reference earlier artifacts (backward traceability)?
- Does the database record for the requirement have a way to point forward to artifacts that will be spawned by the requirement set, such as test cases?

Be wary of adding requirements late in the project.

Each new requirement can disrupt others in ways that are not immediately obvious.

Make sure that your team has extensive discussions before they add a requirement late in the game.

When you add a new requirement, make sure that it does not conflict with any other requirements, or duplicate another one.

Caution: Recognize that there can be serious problems with a list of requirement statements.

Users have trouble fitting all the statements together to imagine the system.

Users may approve the list without anticipating how the system will work, then complain when you deliver something they never imagined.

Also, despite your best efforts, the language may reflect the needs of developers, and their way of thinking, more than the concepts and actions that stakeholders know in their business. The stakeholders may not fully understand what they are agreeing to.

And even developers may overlook some items, or fail to see that two statements disagree.

Checklist for functional requirement statements

Each functional requirement statement is…

Correct

- It is a true statement of what the system must do.
- It is really something the system must do.
- The stakeholders or subject matter experts confirm that this requirement is correct.

Concise

- Appears in a single sentence. (No explanations, arguments, extra comments allowed).

Consistent

- This requirement does not conflict with any other requirements.
- It matches the Vision document.

Functional

- Describes what the system must do, not what the user must do.
- Focuses on function, not user interface. Avoids specifying exactly what the user will see (the user interface) so that the designers have some

freedom of movement. (You will get to the UI when you do a test case).

Unambiguous

- Uses *must* or *shall* as the auxiliary verb.
- Is subject to one and only one interpretation.
- Uses natural language.
- Avoids giving permission (with words such as *may, can, should, could*).
- Uses only one term for a concept, throughout, and that term is defined in the glossary.
- Avoids the normal (words such as *usually, generally, often, or typically*).
- Includes actual measures instead of adjectives that imply a status or value.
- Resists fantasy (such as 100% accuracy).
- Diagrams help illustrate the intent of the requirement.

Verifiable

- This requirement can be tested. (You can measure if this requirement has really been met.)
- The test process is finite and cost effective.

Unique

- There are no other requirements that say the same thing, or almost the same thing. (If so, delete one).

Traceable

- You can trace back from this requirement to the feature and from the feature to the stakeholder request.
- Each requirement has a unique identifier.
- Each requirement can be distinguished from others.

Checklist for the entire set of functional requirement statements

As a group, the collection of requirement statements is...

Complete

- The set describes all the significant requirements of concern to the stakeholders.
- You have included values for all the attributes for each requirement
- You have identified the ranges of input values expected in all possible scenarios.
- You have included responses to both valid and invalid input values.
- All terms are defined in a glossary.
- Any figures, tables, and diagrams include full labels and references.

Modifiable

- You can change the requirements easily, completely, and consistently without losing the style and structure of individual requirements.
- When there are overlapping requirements, they are cross-referenced.

Well organized

- You have grouped related requirements together.
- When several requirements describe a sequence of actions, you put the requirements in chronological order.
- You organize by the logic of a user, not the ID numbers of requirements.

Free of statements that are *not* requirements

- Nothing says how to accomplish these goals in code.
- Nothing says how to test for success.
- Nothing discusses schedule or budget.

Chapter 4. Moving toward use cases

We have gradually moved away from describing requirements in statements, because they so often looked at functions from the point of view of the developers, not the users. The stakeholders often misunderstood what was being planned, got disappointed with the results, and in some situations, refused to accept the deliverables. This approach came to be seen as just too risky. So we turned to use cases.

The **name** of a use case articulates a **goal** that the user wants to achieve, using the functions of the proposed product. Example: Register for a Course.

The **details** of the use case describe, step by step, the actions the user will take to get to that goal, and the responses from the system (its functions).

A use case has two audiences.

The use case describes the proposed functions primarily from the point of view of the **users**, but it also gives the **developers** the specific details they need.

- **Users** find use cases easier to understand than a grab-bag of requirement statements. So when they agree, "Yes, that is what we want the system to do," the developers can feel more confident designing that.

- **Developers** often prefer use cases instead of lists of requirement statements, because the use cases provide meaningful context and detail, showing how functions need to work together to support user tasks, where requirement statements just describe each function in isolation.

Use cases help both stakeholders and developers **imagine** the way that people will use the new system.

And use cases spark better conversations between the developers and representatives of the users. Each group gets to ask, "What do you mean here? And here?" Because use cases provoke a lot of discussion, they get heavily revised, and clarified as everyone moves toward meaningful **agreement**.

It is OK to define functional requirements with both use cases and declarative statements.

Both may be necessary to understand a system of significant complexity. To decide what the right balance should be between them, consider:

- Context of the application

- Client preferences and environment
- Skills of developer organization
- Risks in the project

The more externally observable behavior there is, the more you will rely on use cases to express the functional requirements.

The more user-oriented your development cycle, the more you will rely on use cases, because they are easier to put on the table, for a discussion between the development team and stakeholders.

But for big multi-year projects involving millions of dollars and thousands of stakeholders, you may need to create both the statements and the use cases. Fortunately, such projects are **rare**.

For the moment, let's turn to the process for building use cases.

Start with a use-case model

We can visualize a system's functional requirements as a set of proposed use cases. This model shows the names of the use cases that we will write later, and the user groups who have those goals. The model is a very high-level view of the whole set of use cases to come; we call it a **model**, because we usually show it as a diagram. It just points to the use cases we think need to be written, later.

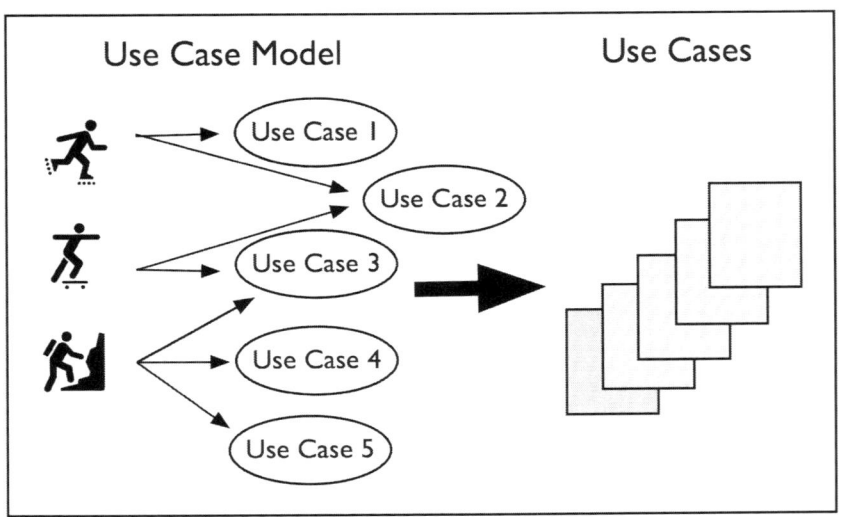

A Use-Case Model represents all the proposed functionality of the new system, at a very high level, way above the nitty-gritty details that will be hammered out when you come to write the actual use cases.

The use-case model shows:

- The major actors
- Their goals
- The other systems that might be involved (such as a database)
- Very brief descriptions of the actions that the user may perform to achieve the goal (a preview of the actual use case)

You might think of the use-case model as a to-do list.

Why create a use-case model?

The use-case model acts as a focus for discussion between the developers and stakeholders.

- Tying stakeholder needs and goals to the functional requirements
- Describing a new system from the point of view of the users
- Identifying who or what will interact with the proposed system
- Showing the most important user roles, such as Teacher and Student
- Naming those users' goals, that is, the tasks they should be able to perform
- Defining the boundaries of the system
- Allowing both developers and stakeholders to refine, verify, and validate the functional requirements for the new system
- Helping the development team plan the work to come

1. Name the people who will use the system

In the use-case model, you are identifying types—roles, not individuals.

- Phone Owner—not Mr. Giovanni Harukami
- Foreign Travel Manager—not Ms. Buckley

Each type of user is thought of as an **actor**.

> Remember: An actor represents a particular type of user, rather than an actual user.

An actor is the person who initiates an interaction, and exchanges data with the system, to achieve a goal, using one or more functions of the new system.

An actor is the person who:

- Requests action
- Provides information
- Retrieves information
- Makes decisions
- Changes information (creating, editing, deleting)

To discover the actor, look at each function and ask:

- Who is using this function?
- Who is launching the actual interaction?
- Who wants to get information from the system?
- Who will be providing information to the system?

Naming the actor

Name the role, not an individual person.

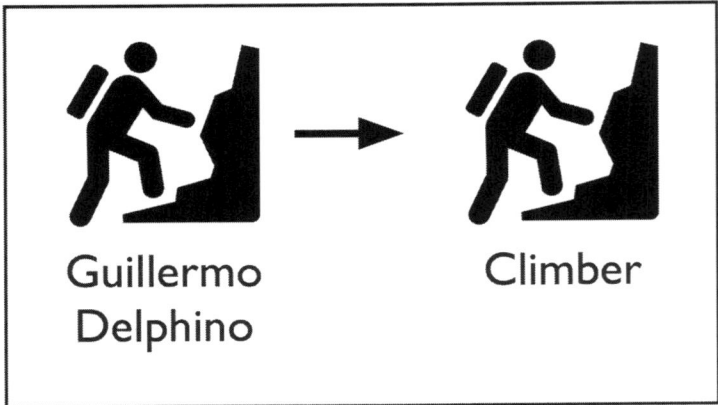

Why?

The actor's name should be generic, describing a role, not an individual.

Distinguish groups when they have different goals, or use different functions.

Why?

When people in different roles use different functions, we need to distinguish between the subgroups, rather than lumping them all together. For example, instead of "employee" we might have two actors: "worker," and "manager."

2. Name the goal of the actor.

The goal becomes the name of a use case. So for each proposed feature, or set of requirements, ask yourself:

- Who is the person who does this or needs it done? (That person is the actor for this use case).
- What is the goal of the person who needs this feature? (That goal becomes the name of the use case.)
- Is this goal important enough that the user will take concrete steps to achieve it? (Those steps will appear in the use case).

Examples of goals:

- Withdraw cash.
- Transfer funds.
- Deposit funds.

Begin each goal with an active verb.

Not: Course registration.

Better: Register for courses.

Take the actor's point of view.

Not: Use our wonderful registration system.

Better: Register for a course.

Tip: Make the name of each goal unique, to distinguish each goal from all others.

A feature hints at the actor's goal, but here we want to state that goal in the actor's own words.

Features are relatively easy to map to use cases—or at least, the names of use cases.

Feature	Goal
People can chat with one member at a time.	Chat with another member.
People can set up a conference call with other members.	Place a conference call.
People can review a chat, reading through the text.	Review a chat.
People can save the text of a chat.	Save a chat.
People can delete the text of a chat.	Delete a chat.

The phrase describing the goal becomes the name of the use case.

One use case may describe one or many requirements.

The use case will describe the steps toward a goal that has meaning for the user. But some requirements are not really goals of the user. They are steps on the way. For instance, very few users say, gosh, I dream of entering a ZIP code. So that is not a use case. It may, however, appear as part of the use case Purchase a Product.

If you are moving from a list of requirement statements to a bunch of use cases, you will usually end up with fewer use cases than requirement statements.

Feel free to demote some requirements to the level of a step, far beneath the notice of the use case name. Remember, the use case name reflects a user's goal, not some trivial action on the way there.

4. Moving toward use cases

3. Put each goal—and nothing else—in an oval.

Later we will describe how the actor accomplishes this goal by using the system. That step-by-step description will appear in the **use case**. But right now we are just identifying the goals that will be fleshed out in the use cases later. Nothing else goes in the oval: no requirements, no numbers.

Examples of use cases in a use-case model

Not so good:

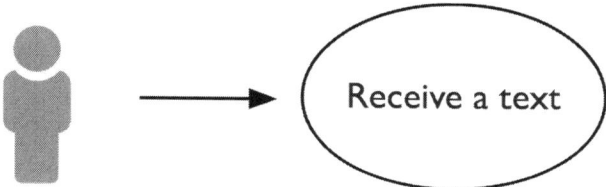

Why not?

There is no user action. And no one just wants to receive a text. People want to read a text, reply to a text, delete a text. Those are goals that can be made into use cases.

Better

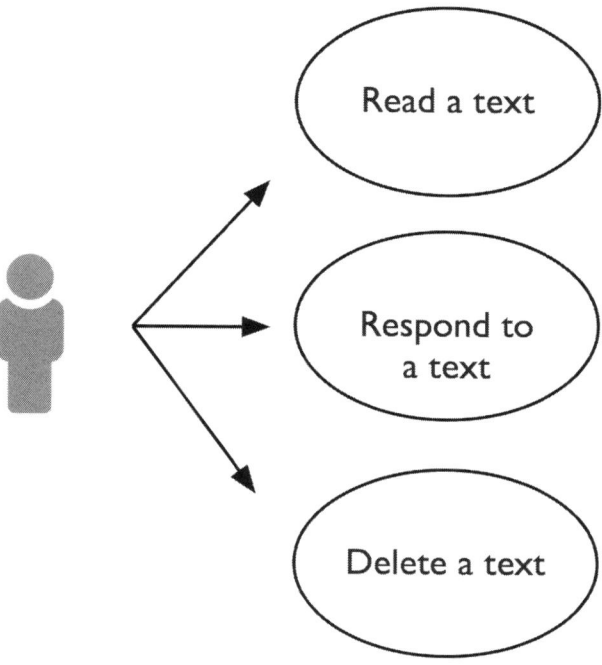

Not so good:

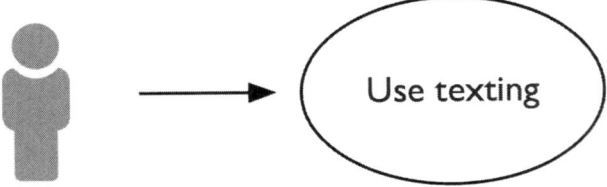

Why not?
"Using" encompasses several user actions, with different goals.

Also, few people think, "Gosh, I want to use my text system." They think: "I want to send a text, respond to a text, include a photo in a text, include a video."

Better:

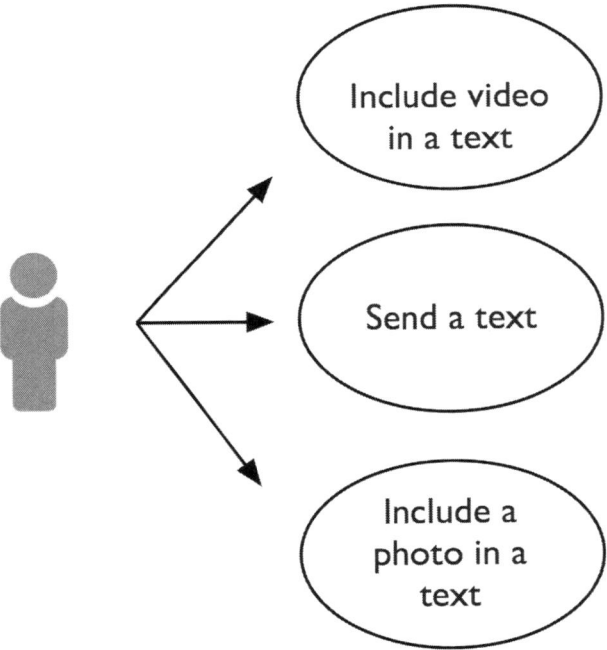

4. Moving toward use cases

Not so good:

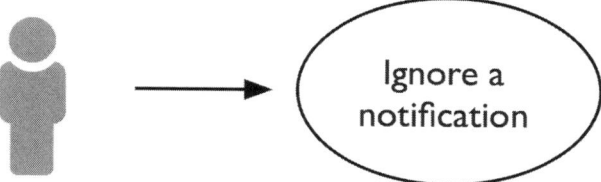

Why not?

Ignoring a notification takes no energy. No one has to do anything to ignore a notification. Because there is no user action on the system, there is no need for a use case.

Not so good:

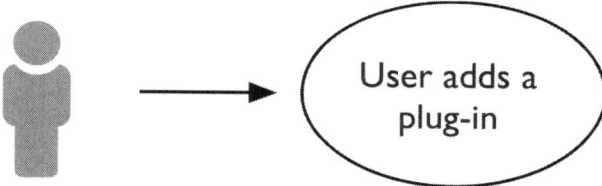

Why not?

The name of the use case does not follow convention. The name should not be a sentence. It should state a goal, beginning with a verb in the imperative: Add a plug-in.

Better:

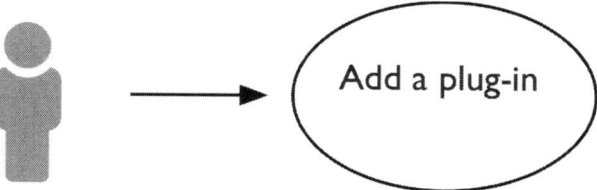

Not so good:

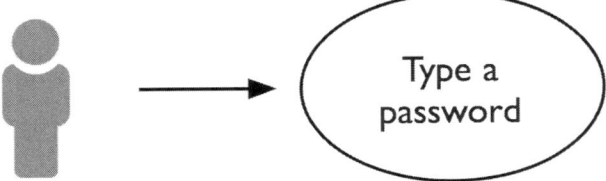

Why not? This action might be part of a use case, but it is not a use case, because it does not represent a real goal of the average user.

Not so good:

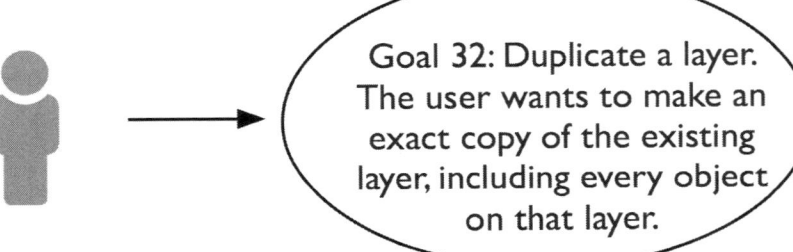

Why not? The name of the use case should not include the Goal Number. In fact, when you create the use case, you are probably too early in the project to start numbering your use cases. And the oval should not include any description of the use case. That could go in a separate, optional section, as a brief description.

Better:

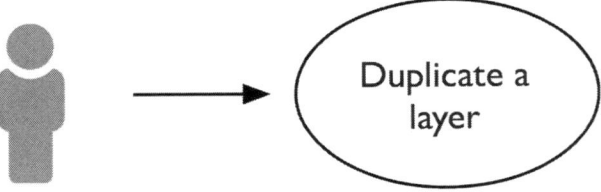

4. Moving toward use cases

4. Connect the actor with one or more goals.

In the diagram, draw a line from the actor to the goal.

You are setting up a **relationship** between the actor and the use case. In effect, the actor now owns the use case.

For each actor, identify all the goals that person has, in regard to the system.

To collect all the goals of an actor, ask:

- Why does this actor want to use the system?
- Will this actor create, store, change, remove, or read data in the system? If so, why?
- Will the actor need to inform the system about external events?
- Must the actor be informed about occurrences within the system?

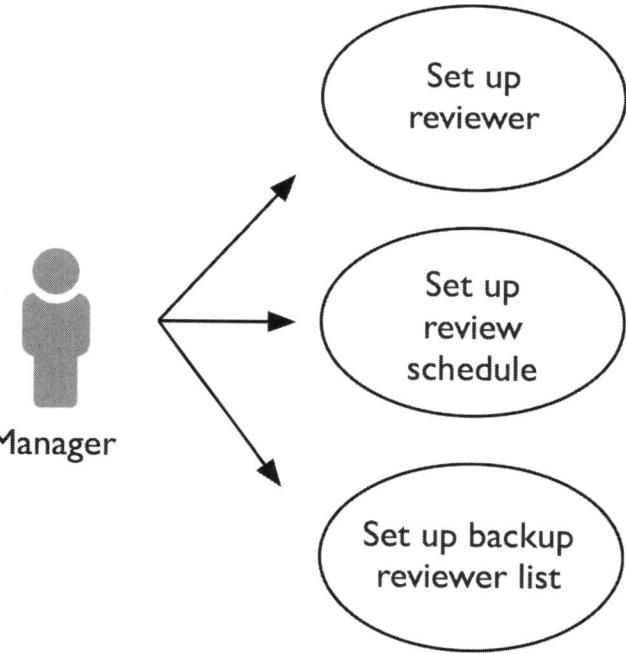

5. For each use case, identify any other systems that the system must talk to.

When the actor launches a function in our system, pursuing a goal, the system may need to get info from **another system** or **a database**. That other system is considered an actor, though inhuman and secondary. Examples:

- A hardware device (such as a monitoring station)
- A database
- Another program (such as a mapping application)

To discover non-human actors in a use case, ask:

What hardware device, subsystem, or database responds to signals or messages from our new system?

In other words, if we are building a widget, and that widget may need to send a request to a monitoring station to find out what the current temperature is, that station would be a secondary actor in the use case.

Example:

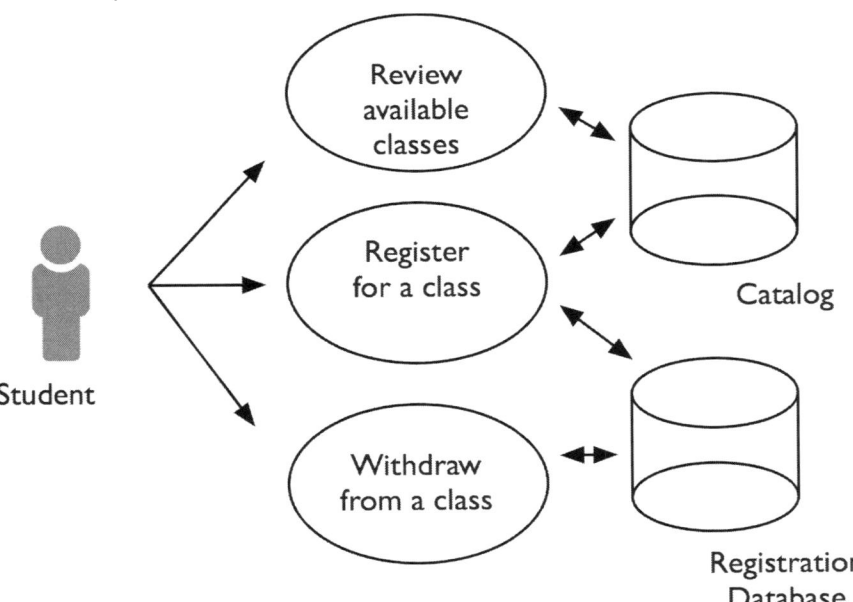

- In a list, the student chooses a course. The system looks up the course in the Catalog and displays that information to the student, with the option to enroll.

4. Moving toward use cases

- The student chooses to register for the course.
- The system sends that information to the Registration Database and displays a confirmation for the student.
- Later, the student chooses to withdraw from the course.
- The system sends that information to the Registration Database and displays a confirmation for the student.

6. Organize the set of use cases in a way that makes sense to key stakeholders.

Put all the use cases for a major actor together.

Tip: Organize these use cases in rough chronological order, if possible.

If you have a lot of use cases, group some into packages.

In a use-case model, a package may contain:

- Use cases and their actors
- A set of actors who belong to a particular department or task area
- Smaller packages

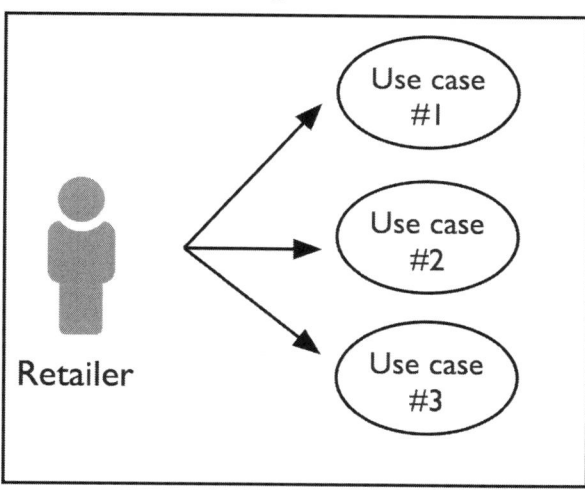

Package 2

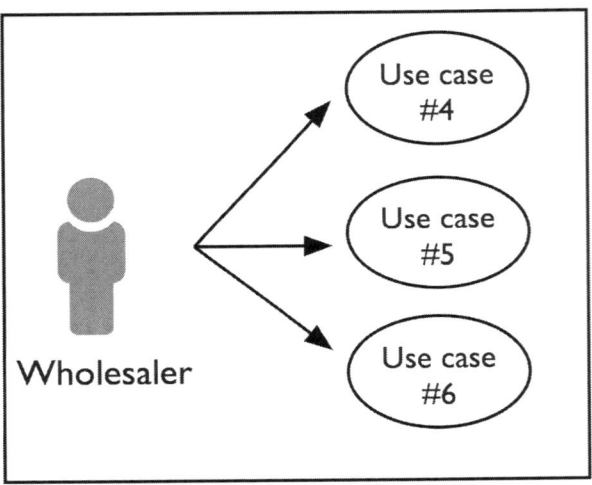

Package 3

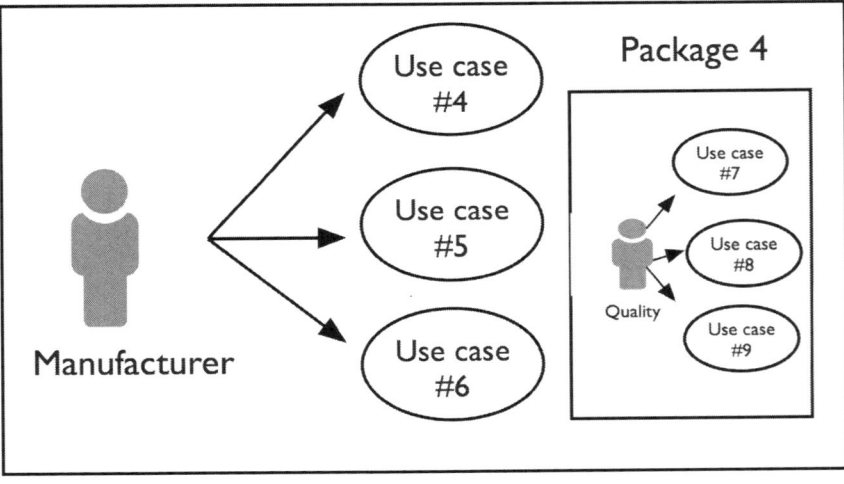

7. (Optional) Write a brief description of each use case.

Use a description to capture the discussion in the brainstorming sessions, and interviews with stakeholders.

These are not formal descriptions. They are designed to give people a basic idea of the purpose, and flow.

Brief descriptions mention the main actions that the user takes, and the main responses of the system. Briefly!

They do not get into options, choices, errors, or details.

Examples of brief descriptions

Brief descriptions of three use cases for a proposed Registration System:

Register for a Course

The student chooses to register for courses. The system displays a list of departments, campuses, and semesters. The student chooses a department, a campus, and a semester. The system then pulls the list of those courses from the Course Catalog system. The student picks a course and completes registration.

Register for Housing

The student chooses to register for housing. The system displays the housing choices available to the student, based on the student's registration status (full time or part time). The student asks for information about one of the housing choices, and the system fetches that information from the Housing System. The student picks a housing choice, and the system checks on availability from the Housing System. When availability is confirmed, the student registers for that housing. The system sends a confirming email to the student.

Sign Up for Parking

The student chooses to sign up for parking. The system displays the set of parking lots with available slots, drawn from the Parking Assignment System. The student picks a lot, and the system confirms that choice.

Good and bad brief descriptions

Not so good:

```
Open a recent file

The user logs into the system and chooses to
open recent files. The system displays the
last ten files used. The user picks one, and
the system opens it.
```

What's wrong here?

The description suggests that you can only open a recent file if you log into the system first. But in reality, you can open a recent file even if you have already logged in and done some other stuff.

Moral: Just focus on the functionality of the use case.

Better:

```
Open a recent file

The user chooses to open recent files. The
system displays the last ten files used. The
user picks one, and the system opens it.
```

Not so good:

```
Place an Image

The user wants to bring an image from another
file, putting it into a new layer in the
current document. The user goes to the File
menu and chooses the option to Place Image or
⌘-Option-I. The system displays the file
handling dialog. The user picks the file and
clicks the Open button. The system places the
image into a new layer in the current
document.
```

What's wrong here?

The description defines elements of the user interface. But we should leave those undefined at this point. We want the team to be free to define the user interface, including menu items, and shortcuts, at a later date. So we avoid saying what the actual buttons, menu items, and icons are.

Also, the description talks about the actor's inner life, describing the user's desire. In a use case, we do not speculate on the subjective experience. The name of the use case expresses the goal. That is enough for now.

Better:

```
Place an Image on a New Layer
```

```
To bring an image from another file, putting
it into a new layer in the current document,
the user chooses the option to place the
image. The system displays the file handling
dialog. The user picks the file and chooses to
place it as an image. The system places the
image into a new layer in the current
document.
```

8. Review the use-case model.

In a series of group meetings you need to discuss and modify the evolving draft of the use-case model with representatives of the users and developers.

Does the name of each use case reflect a real goal of the user?

- Key: The name starts with a verb in the imperative, followed by a noun describing the object that the user wants to work with.

- The use case focuses on one goal, not several, and not some vague agglomeration of goals, such as "Manage all settings."

- The noun is singular. "Put an employee on an action plan," rather than putting several employees, or all employees, all at once, on notice.

- If the user wants to do several different things with the same object, build a use case for each goal, such as Create a contact, Delete a contact, Make a contact into a favorite.

Can the users understand it?

- Is it easy for real users to understand what the new system will do for them, by reviewing this model?

- Do customers, users, and developers all understand the names and brief descriptions?

- Do your packages contain meaningful groups of related use cases, or sets of actors?

- If you have brief descriptions, do they give a true picture of the use cases?

Is the model complete?

- Have all use cases been identified?
- Is every functional requirement represented here, either in its own use case, or as part of a larger use case?
- Do these use cases collectively account for all required behavior?
- For every feature, is there at least one use case?

Is the model efficient?

- Have you eliminated any superfluous use cases—ones that do not trace back to a feature, or functional requirement?
- Are there similar or redundant use cases that can be deleted?
- Does each use case have a unique, intuitive, and explanatory name, so that they cannot be mixed up later?
- Is at least one actor involved with each use case?

Are all use cases at the same level?

- Do you have several levels of use cases? (The ones at the lower levels are probably just steps.)
- If you have a lot of little use cases, ask yourself whether they should be merged.

Do the use cases lead to measurable results?

- Does this particular activity lead to a real end result that someone wants?
- Is the result measurable? Could a neutral observer point to a tangible result, a visible change in the state of the system?
- Will we be able to prove success?

Caution: Avoid functional decomposition.

Avoid breaking down a feature into many small, isolated parts.

- The parts are supposed to work together to provide the function.
- But, seen in isolation, each part is meaningless.

Functional Decomposition identifies the steps, separately, but not the sequence.

4. Moving toward use cases

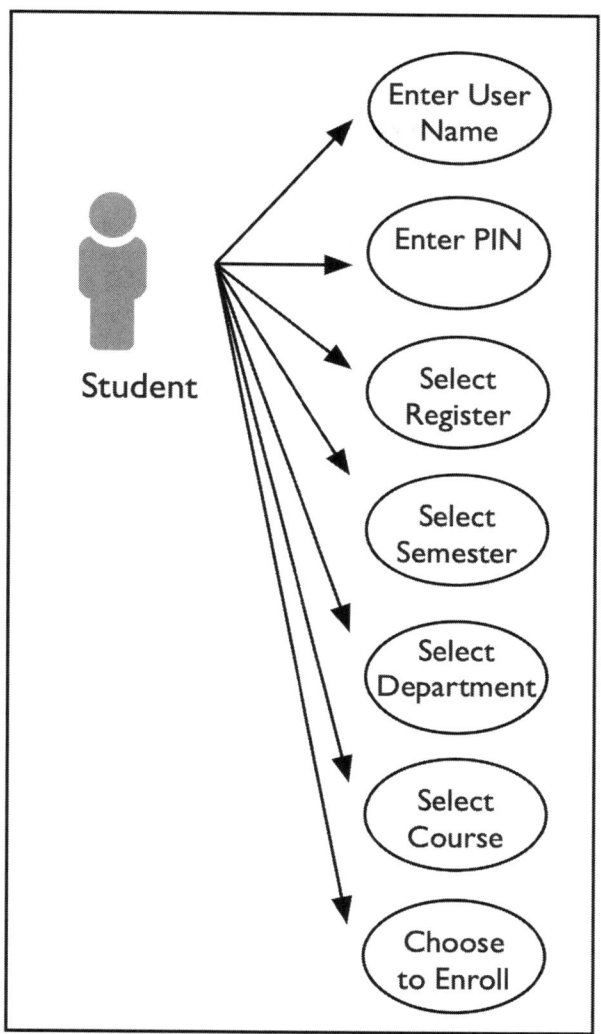

Problems

- These proposed use cases do not reflect real user goals.
- Each function lacks context.
- Stakeholders have to cross-reference a bunch of these pieces, and, failing that, they get a very fragmented idea of the system.
- The goals of the actor are not clear.

- Developers cannot see the relationship between the requirements.
- Developers have to write more code; ergo, there are more bugs.
- Testers have to write a test script for each step, but there is no end-to-end test of what the system must do.

Symptoms of functional decomposition:

- Lots of very small use cases
- Use cases with no result of value
- Names with low-level operations, such as Insert Card.

To escape functional decomposition, ask:

- Why are we building this part of the system?
- What does the user want to achieve?
- Whose goal does this satisfy?
- What value does this use case add?
- What is the story behind this use case?

Use cases are not functional decompositions.

- They keep the functionality together to describe a complete use of the system.
- Each use case provides a context for its sequence of steps.
- The use case describes a task that produces a result that is of value to the actor.

Chapter 5. Creating a use case

A use case expresses one or more functional requirements in a way that users can understand, and engineers can implement. A use case works better than a bunch of requirement statements.

What's wrong with requirement statements?

Stakeholders have trouble understanding what they will be able to do with the new system, based on dozens or hundreds of separate statements.

- The requirement statements are not arranged according to what a user might do.
- It is hard to find all the requirements that might relate to the actions a user would perform to get to a particular goal.
- It is very hard to tell if anything has been left out.
- The terms may be ones that make sense to programmers, but not to ordinary users.
- Most people do not think this way.

Even programmers have a hard time understanding what they are supposed to develop, based on a set of requirement statements.

- For any given requirement, the programmer has no context: Why does the user want this? What is the goal?
- One programmer may work on one requirement, while others work on related ones…but when their code is complete, the modules do not work together…because no one understood what the user was trying to do.
- Having a lot of individual requirement statements can lead to focusing on just one requirement at a time, ignoring the others…so that in the end you meet all the requirements, but the program does not do what users need it to do.

Ivar Jacobson suggested use cases as a solution.

Instead of giving the stakeholders a laundry list of requirements, he suggested describing business processes as stories, with actors such as customers, and objects such as products.

He was making the case for an object-oriented approach to programming, in books like *Object-Oriented Software Engineering - A Use Case Driven Approach* (1992) and *The Object Advantage* (1994).

As object-oriented programming came to dominate the industry, use cases proliferated, particularly on large projects.

The approach is now common.

But the way people build use cases varies from group to group. There is no one way to make a use case.

Martin Fowler says:

> There is no standard way to write the content of a use case, and different formats work well in different cases. —*UML Distilled* (Third Edition). Addison-Wesley, 2004.

Alistair Cockburn offers several versions in his book *Writing Effective Use Cases* (2001), such as the "casual" and the "fully dressed" flavors.

Here is a full example of a use case.

Example of a use case

Insurance15: Start a claim for loss

Brief Description:

The clerk chooses to start a new claim. The system requests the policy number. The clerk enters that. The system displays policy information, including the types of claims that can be made against the policy. The clerk identifies the claim type and enters information about the claim. The system verifies that information and provides a list of adjusters. The clerk picks one. The system offers the clerk an opportunity to review the entire claim. The clerk does so, and submits the claim. The system notifies the agent, the customer, and the adjuster, and stores the claim in the claims database.

Actors

- The claims clerk
- The claims database
- The policy database
- The customer database
- The agent database
- The adjusters database

Preconditions

The clerk is logged into the Claim Capture program.

The network is live.

The program has access to the databases, and they are functioning.

Scenarios

The clerk creates a new claim in the system: Basic Flow

The power goes out: Basic Flow, Power Failure.

No such policy: Basic Flow, Policy Number Not Found.

No coverage: Basic Flow, Policy Does Not Cover Loss

Clerk reviews and edits: Basic Flow, Edits During Review

Clerk fails to submit: Basic Flow, No Submission

Basic flow

1. On the home page of the application, the clerk chooses to start a new claim.	The system requests the policy number.
2. The clerk enters the policy number.	The system displays current policy information, and the types of claims that can be made against the policy.
3. The clerk chooses Loss as the type of claim.	The system displays a form with the policy number, customer name and contact information, insurance agent, and fields for date of incident, location street, city, and ZIP, description of incident, claimant, customer estimate of value at loss.
4. The clerk fills in those fields and chooses to submit.	The system verifies that there are valid values in each field, and then assigns a claim number. It displays a list of adjusters near the location of the incident.

5. The clerk selects an adjuster and chooses to assign that adjuster to the claim.	The system verifies availability of the adjuster, confirms assignment, and offers the clerk the option to review the claim before finalizing it.
6. The clerk agrees to review the claim.	The system displays all the information about the claim.
7. The clerk reviews the information and chooses Submit.	The system confirms submission, stores the information in the claims database, sends notices to the agent, the customer, and the adjuster, and returns the clerk to the welcome screen. The use case ends.

Alternate Flows

A1: Power Failure. System autosaves at each commit point. Use case ends.

A2: Policy Number Not Found. In step 2, the system does not find the policy number in the database, and notifies the clerk. The use case ends.

A3: Policy does not cover loss. In step 2, the loss type does not appear in this policy. Clerk notifies agent and customer. Use case ends.

A4: Edits During Review. The clerk decides to change something that was entered. To do so, the clerk chooses to Edit that section, and the system returns the clerk to that screen. The use case continues from that step.

A5: No Submission. The clerk fails to submit. After five minutes of inactivity, the system autosaves the information, but does not mark the claim as submitted. The system blocks access to the current screen, posting a login request in front of it. The use case ends.

Post condition

The new claim is now in the database; notices have been sent to the agent, the customer, and the adjuster.

What is a use case?

Formal definition:

A use case defines a sequence of **actions** performed by an **actor** and the **system** yielding an observable **result** of value to an actor.

A sequence of actions

- Each **action** is performed fully—or not at all.
- The actions performed by the system are the **functional requirements**.

With an observable result of value

If nobody receives value from the use case, then the use case is probably too small.

(Combine it with others, as a step toward a real goal for an actor).

To an actor

Decide which particular actor receives the **value**. (Narrow your focus).

Usually the actor getting the value is also the one who **initiates** the sequence of actions.

Even if several actors are involved, the primary actor is the one **receiving the value**.

If no one receives value, you may not have a use case. You may just be describing some small function of the system. Incorporate it into a real use case.

If more than one actor receives value, your use case may be too large. (Doing too much for too many actors).

One big use case could do everything for everyone. For example: Operate the Registration System. But that is hard to follow.

Break it up into a bunch of smaller use cases.

A use case describes:

- How actors interact with the system to reach a goal
- What the system should do in response (the desired functionality)

In this way, a use case groups together all requirements related to a particular actor achieving a particular goal in a single story.

- The use case is a **complete** and **meaningful** flow of events from the perspective of a particular actor (the one whose goal is achieved).
- It describes what the actor does, and how the system responds. Each line shows the actor doing something, and the system doing something in response.
- Each step, then, shows the functionality that the actor will use. Each function is a requirement. That's why a use case is one way to describe functional requirements.
- At the conclusion of the last step the actor reaches a goal that has some value—for the actor. That goal is announced in the title of the use case.

We build use cases because...

We want to establish a context for the requirements. From a user's perspective, use cases:

- Put a series of system requirements in a logical sequence.
- Collect all the requirements that relate to the user accomplishing this particular task.
- Show how the requirements help the user accomplish a goal.
- Show why the system is needed.
- Help users verify that all requirements have been captured.

Everyone can understand them.

- You use terms that customers and users understand.
- You are telling a concrete story about using the system.
- You can verify that all stakeholders understand—and agree.

Use cases help customers verify the requirements and agree to proceed.

Use cases give developers a spec they can build from.

The use case answers a developer's questions, such as:

- What is the situation before these events begin? (Preconditions)
- What does the actor do?
- How does the system respond?
- What information gets exchanged?
- What is the situation after these events have played out? (Post Conditions)

Use cases form the basis for discussion between the developers and the stakeholders.

The development team talks about the use case with representatives of the stakeholders, particularly the users, to see what they think.

As both groups discuss and modify the model and the use cases, they try to reach agreement on what to develop.

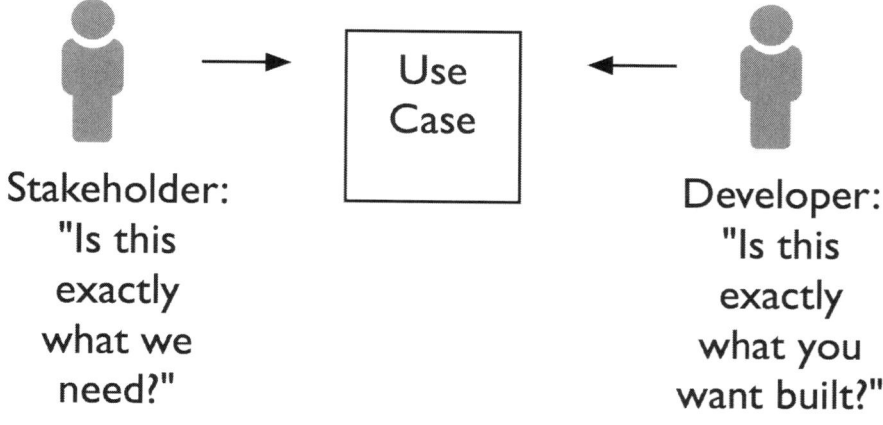

Stakeholder: "Is this exactly what we need?"

Developer: "Is this exactly what you want built?"

Extended example: A full use case

UC23: Register for One or More Courses

Status

> Draft

Brief Description

> The student enters the system and chooses to register for courses. The system allows the student to choose a department, a campus, and a semester. The system then pulls the list of courses from the Course Catalog system. The student picks up to six courses, and completes registration.

Actors

- Student
- Course Catalog system
- Registration database

Special Requirements

> The system must validate or reject a schedule within one minute of the time that the student submits it.

Preconditions

- The system has communication with the Course Catalog System.
- The list of courses for the semester has been created in the Course Catalog System.
- The student has already set up an account. On login, the system confirms that he or she is a currently enrolled student, with no outstanding charges.

Scenarios (and Alternative Scenarios)

- Register for courses: Basic Flow
- Unidentified student: Basic Flow, Unidentified Student
- Quit before registering: Basic Flow, Quit
- Cannot enroll: Basic Flow, Cannot Enroll.
- Registration closed: Basic Flow, Registration Closed.

5. Creating a use case

- Course Catalog System Unavailable: Basic Flow, Course Catalog System Unavailable

Basic Flow

Step	Student Action	System Response
1. Log On	Student opens the system's welcome page.	The system asks for identification.
	Student enters a valid User ID and password.	System validates the ID and password, and displays the registration page, with menu of options, including Create a Schedule.
2. Select Create a Schedule	Student chooses Create a Schedule.	The system asks for the campus, semester, and department.
3. Obtain course information.	The student enters the campus, semester, and department.	The system displays a list of course titles, drawn from the Course Catalog System.
4. Select a course.	The student selects a course.	The system adds that to the student's schedule, and offers to display a list of courses for the same department, or another one.
	The student continues to select courses, up to a maximum of six.	
5. Submit schedule	The student submits the schedule.	The system verifies that the courses do not overlap or conflict on times. For each course, the system verifies that the student has the prerequisites, that the course has open slots. The system enrolls the student in each course. The system displays the completed schedule, with a confirmation number and request to confirm.
6. Confirm schedule	The student confirms the completed schedule.	The system saves the student's registrations for each course in the Registration database. The use case ends.

Alternative Flows

Alt 1: Unidentified Student

> In Step 1, Log On, the system discovers that the student ID and password combination is not valid, so the system displays an error message. The use case ends.

Alt 2: Quit

> If the student chooses to quit, at any time after Step 4, the system asks if the student wants to save a partial schedule before quitting. All courses in which the student is already enrolled are marked Enrolled. Any courses that the student selected, but did not enroll in, are marked Selected. If the student approves of saving the schedule, it is saved. The use case ends.

Alt 3: Course Catalog System Unavailable

> In Step 3, Obtain Course Information, in the Basic Flow, if the system is unable to communicate with the Course Catalog System, it displays an error message to the student. The student acknowledges the message. The use case ends.

Alt 4: Cannot Enroll

> In Step 5, Submit Schedule, the system discovers that a course conflicts with the time of another, or that the student does not have the prerequisites for the course, so the system will not enroll the student in the course. A message appears suggesting that the student pick another course. The use case continues at Step 4, Select Courses, in the Basic Flow.

Alt 5: Registration Closed

> In Step 1, Log On, if the student signs in successfully at a time when enrolment has not yet opened, or has already been closed, the system displays a message saying so. The use case ends.

Extension Points

> None.

Post Conditions

> The student is enrolled in one or more courses with a confirmed schedule, and the system has saved the registrations.

5. Creating a use case

Diagram

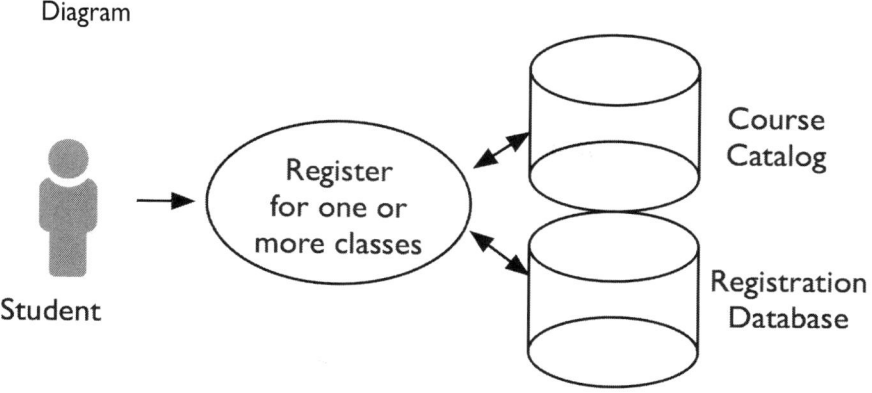

How is a use case different from a procedure?

A use case is like a procedure in some ways:

- It describes the actions that a user (the actor) takes, to reach a particular goal.
- It describes the way the system responds.
- It is complete. If all goes well, the actor achieves the goal.

But unlike a procedure, a use case…

- Describes an **imagined** system, not a real one.

    (We are building use cases as we gather requirements, before we build the product).

- Acts as a **container** for a number of functional requirements (things the software must do).

    Each system response is, in essence, a functional requirement.

- Talks **in the third person** about what the actor does, and what the system does.

    You do not give direct orders. You do not write in the imperative. You are creating a narrative.

- Includes information that is mostly of use to the **developers**.

    The system state before the action begins (preconditions).

    Every system response to user actions, in every step.

    All the scenarios, including errors, exceptions, options—paths that may be mentioned in passing in procedures, but that get full attention in a use case.

    The system state at the end (post conditions).

- Does not describe a particular interface.

    The interface is still to be designed, so the use case tends to be vague about just how the user does things. That's on purpose.

    You do not say click x, pick this tab, or push the yellow button. You are agnostic about what the screen will look like.

    The developers may need to develop for several different devices: a computer, a touchscreen tablet, a smartphone…so the interfaces may be different, but they all have to allow the same actions. Your job is to describe what the user is doing—in abstract terms.

You cannot start talking about a particular menu item, or box, because they do not exist, and your job in the use case is **not** to predict what those elements of the user interface will be. They come later. A specialist creates a user interface spec, to define those things.

A use case lays the basis for other artifacts, such as test cases and procedures. For example, a use case may form the basis for a test case.

- The test case spells out the actions the user must take, and the responses expected from the system.
- The test case moves closer to a real procedure, because it specifies parts of an actual user interface to be used.
- The test case is often written from a user's point of view, giving direct instructions.

A use case may also form the basis for a procedure.

- The essential actions are here.
- But you cannot write the procedure until you see an actual interface.
- In writing the procedure, you discover how the designers handled these actions, and how the developers built those designs, in an actual product.

But the audiences differ.

The audience for a use case is twofold:

> **Stakeholders**, who review use cases to make sure that the team understands what they want the system to do.
>
> **Developers**, who read use cases to find out what they should build.

The audience for a procedure is just **the user**.

> Yes, there may be users with differing skills, interests, experiences.
>
> But you are writing for all of them.
>
> You are not writing a procedure for the developers.

The purposes also differ:

> You write a use case so that the stakeholders and developers can go through it, talk about it, verify it, and finally agree. You write use cases so that the team can develop useful software.

You write a procedure so that one or more users can accomplish their goals, using the software. By the time you write a procedure, the code has already been written, and there is a visible user interface.

The elements of the use case

The use case sits in the middle of a discussion between the stakeholders and the development team. We draft a use case to facilitate that discussion.

The discussion is more important, more revealing, more helpful than the use case itself.

We constantly revise the use case so that it records the answers to the questions that get hashed out, documenting the understanding between all parties.

Each element in a standard use case is designed to answer a particular type of question.

What use case are we talking about?

> Elements: ID and Name. (The ID is a unique code to identify this particular use case. The name identifies a user goal.)

Where do we stand on this use case?

> Element: Status. (Is this a draft? Final?)

What happens in this use case?

> Element: Brief description. (What happens, in skeletal form).

Who are the players?

> Element: Actors (Who initiates, benefits from the use case)

What business rules or requirement statements does this use case enact?

> Element: Requirements. (Optional section with rules or requirement statements that relate to the actions here).

What are we assuming about the system state before we start the use case?

> Element: Preconditions. (What the system must be like before we begin.)

What are the different possible paths through these actions?

> Element: Scenarios. (Narratives of different paths through the possible actions.)

What is the flow of events when all goes well?

> Element: Basic Flow. (Sequences of actions showing what the actor does, and what the system does in response.)

Is there some sequence of steps that happens here and in other use cases?

Element: Subflow. (Steps that can be reused in several different use cases.)

What happens when an error occurs, or the user deviates from the basic flow?

Element: Alternate Flow. (Detours or optional paths.)

In the Basic Flow, where could the user stray from the regular path?

Element: Extension Point. (Optional place in the basic flow where a user might go off on a tangent choosing an option other than the regular one).

After the user has successfully completed all the steps in the Basic Flow, what is the state of the system?

Element: Post conditions. (What the developer needs to do after the sue case is complete; the state of the system afterward).

Is there a diagram of the way this works?

Element: Diagram. (A picture of the flow, or the image from the use case model).

Organizing a use case

There is no set standard for what components you must include, or in what order. But here are the most common elements, in the usual order, along with the rarely used elements, where they might appear.

Common   Rare

Common	Rare
ID	
Name	
	Status
Brief Description	
Actors	
	Requirements
Preconditions	
Scenarios	
Basic Flow	
	Subflow
Alternative Flow	
	Extension Points
Post conditions	
	Diagram

Good news: You derive some of this content from earlier documents.

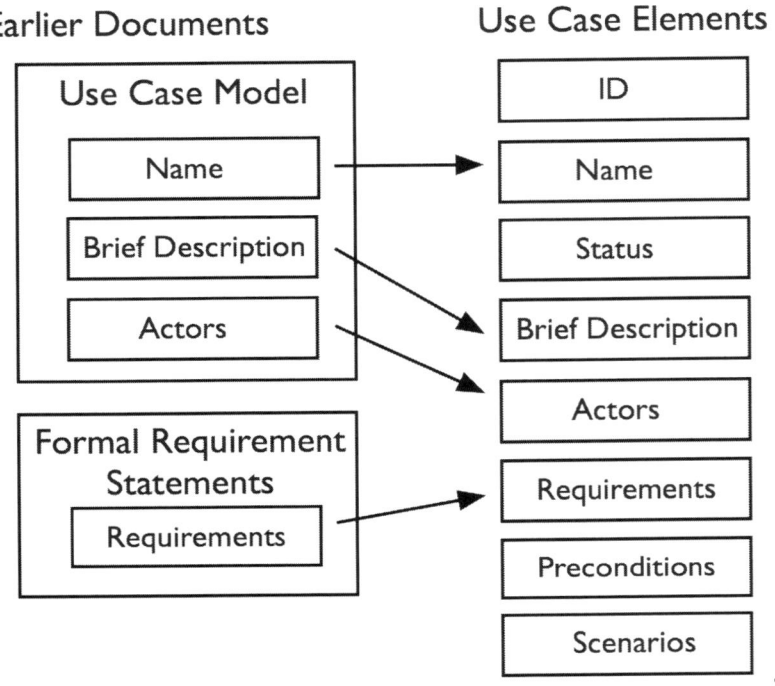

But the core of the use case is the Basic Flow, which is new.

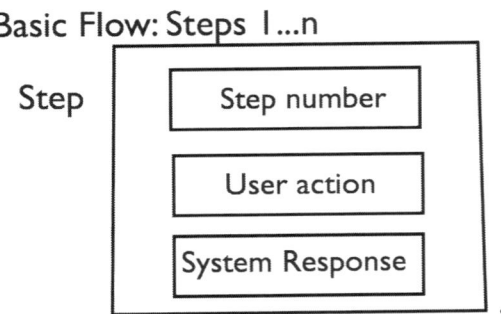

The basic flow consists of one or more steps. Each step describes one action that the actor takes, provoking one or more responses from the system. Every other element revolves around, supports, modifies, impacts the Basic Flow.

1. Create a Name that reflects a goal or purpose of the primary actor.

You have already created the name in your use-case model.

Confirm that the name is easy to distinguish from the names of other use cases.

Confirm that the name meets these criteria:

- Begins with an active verb in the imperative.

    Not: Course registration.

    Better: Register for courses.

- Indicates one value or goal of the actor.

    Good example: Deposit a check.

    Bad example: Format a document. (Encompasses too many actions, each of which might be a use case on its own, such as Change the font on selected text, Create a style, Modify a style, and so on.)

- Focuses on one object, not many (to make testing easier).

- Takes the actor's point of view (to help users understand the steps).

    Not: Use registration system.

    Better: Register for courses.

Correct bad names for use cases, like this:

Making deposits => Make a deposit.

Table creation mechanism => Create a table.

Playlist => Add a song to a playlist.

How to choose a template => Choose a template.

Adjusting the caps on your lines => Adjust the cap on a line.

2. Start tracking its Status. (Optional)

If you have a lot of use cases, and you need to track progress in developing the detailed versions, choose a set of status values, and assign one to the use case now.

The values for the status vary a lot from one company to another, and the correspondence between them is only partial.

One approach describes the progress this way:

- In this view, when you identify a use case, you create the Façade, a kind of placeholder, showing the name, perhaps an actor, and a brief description, as in the Use-Case Model.

- Then you fill in the details, or go some of the way toward that, in the Filled-In version.

- Then you pick a few use cases to focus on, and the ones that are picked are Focused.

- Finally you complete the use case, and its status is, you guessed it, Complete. (The difference between Filled In and Complete is a matter of conjecture.)

In another approach, you start off in Discovery, finding the use cases, giving them names, perhaps actors and relationships. Then you do an Outline of the steps. Then you move through Drafts, where you do some but not all of the flows in detail. Finally, at the end of this process, the use case is Complete.

Some teams try to tie a use case to a particular iteration. But you may only design and implement one of the flows in this iteration. So really, you need to assign each flow to a particular iteration. And the iteration does not really tell you the status of the use case.

> In iterative development it is often difficult to assign an overall status to a use case because its flows may be developed in different iterations.

Status is a pain to define and update, so if you can possibly skip this element, do so.

3. Edit the Brief Description.

Edit the description from the use-case model so that your text describes actions taken by the actors, and does not talk about "the use case."

Before:

> The use case allows a Registrar to close the registration process. Course offerings that do not have enough students are cancelled. The Billing System is notified for each student in each course offering that is not cancelled, so the student can be billed for the course offering.

After

> The Registrar closes the registration process. The system now cancels course offerings that do not have enough students. The system notifies the Billing System for each student in each course offering that is not cancelled, so the student can be billed for the course offering.

Focus on the basic purpose and flow. The description is not a formal mechanism, so it does not have to mention everything that happens, or could happen.

Just describe what the user does—and what the system does in response.

> Include the major actions that the user takes, and the major responses from the system, leading up to the user's goal.

Good Example:

> The user selects an area of the image. The system surrounds that area with highlighting. The user chooses to increase the brightness of that area by a certain percentage. The system shows what that area would look like at that brightness. The user approves, and the brightness is now applied to that area.

Good Example:

> The student chooses to register for courses. The system allows the student to choose a department, a campus, and a semester. The system then goes to the Course Catalog system and pulls the list of courses from the that department, on that campus, during that semester. The student picks up to six courses, and completes registration.

Good Example:

> The student chooses to sign up for parking. The system displays the set of parking lots with available slots, drawn from the Parking Assignment System. The student picks a parking lot, and the system confirms that choice.

Bad Example:

> **Not this**: The user wants to draw a picture of a truck, and to do that, wants to use the line tool.
>
> **What's wrong with this?** The text describes two goals for the user, not one. And of those two goals, one is too specific (a truck) and the other goal is from the programmer's perspective (using the line tool, as opposed to drawing a line).
>
> **Better**: To draw a straight line, the user selects the line tool, moves it to the drawing area; the system changes the tool icon to a plus sign. The user drags it across the plane. The system displays a solid straight line. In the Appearance panel, the user adjusts the width of the stroke, adjusts the cap, and changes the solid line to dashes. After each change, the system modifies the line.

4. List the Actors.

In building the Use-Case Model, you identified the primary actor, the one who triggers the action, and gets the reward from the use case.

Generally, you do not need to describe the actors here—just name the ones involved in the use case. (Often you have only one actor).

> If you need to describe the actors in detail, do so elsewhere—in the Vision document, for example, or as an appendix to the Use-Case Model.
>
> You do not need the stick figures you used in the Use-Case Model. Just the names.

If you have several people acting in the use case, put the primary actor first, as the initiator.

> The Primary Actor is the one who gets value from the use case.
>
> The name of the use case reflects a goal, wish, or need of the Primary Actor—something that any other actors in the use case really do not care a lot about.
>
> The Primary Actor is a human being.

Decide whether to include the actors who are actually just other systems. (Some teams leave these inanimate actors out of the list).

> Remember: An actor is someone or something **outside the system**, acting in a role that interacts with the system. So a list of actors may include systems as well as humans.
>
> **Shorthand definition**: An actor is a person or thing that exchanges data with the system.

You do not need to mention the system that you are developing.

> You are **within** that system. You are not outside of it, sending messages to it, so your own system is not usually listed as an actor.
>
> Whenever the user performs an action, your system is going to respond. You do not have to name it as an actor; that's assumed.
>
> Example: If you are developing a new function for Google Maps, you may have a primary user, or actor, who is a Cartographer, but you do not have to list Google Maps as an actor.

Time to reconsider:

> If you realize that no one really receives any value from the use case, you may need to drop the use case. You are probably looking at a step within some other use case.
>
> If you realize that several different actors receive different values from the use case, ask yourself if you have perhaps combined several use cases into one. Now is a good time to split them up.
>
> Goal: You should have one Primary Actor. Everyone else ought to be a bit-part player.
>
> It is OK for several different actors to receive the same value from the same use case. If you feel uncomfortable picking one of them to initiate the use case, as the Primary Actor, then consider generalizing, inventing a super-actor who represents the others.

Confirm that the actor's name describes a role, or a class of people, not a particular individual, or an all-purpose "user." Test: Could several different individuals play this role?

Remember: One individual can act in more than one role.

5. Insert a Requirements section only if circumstances warrant. (Optional)

Sometimes your team needs to include some of the following:

Features that, however vague, refer to something in the use case.

> The relationship is not always very clear, so the same feature description might land in several use cases.

Functional requirements statements that correspond to this use case.

> Remember that the theory is that most functional requirements should appear as steps in the use case, when you describe what the system does in response to the actors.
>
> In the flow, each system behavior is a functional requirement.
>
> The sequence gives context.
>
> So, technically, you do not need to mention the corresponding requirement statements. And in many projects, the whole idea of separate statements for requirements is anathema, because most developers prefer the use cases.
>
> (If the same requirement statement applies to several use cases, you have to drop it into all of them.)
>
> And if declarative statements do not fit in any use case, or if they apply to the whole system, move them to a section such as Supplementary Specifications.

Change requests

> If you are trying to show customers that you have responded to their requests, you can put their actual requests into a Requirements section, along with any relevant requirements that grew out of those. Why do so? To show stakeholders that the use case is designed to implement what they asked for.

Business rules that correspond to this use case.

> We have not dealt with business rules. They are hard to distinguish from functional requirements statements. If there is a difference, you could say that a business rule focuses on what the business does, and the requirement expresses that in a statement about the system. But most teams have trouble sticking to the distinction.

Special requirements

In a pure form, these are special because they are requirements that are somehow related to this use case, but not covered in the flow of events.

But there should not be many functional requirements that are not described in steps.

So truly "special" requirements should be rare.

You generally do not include any non-functional requirements here because they apply to the whole system, not just this use case, and they focus on issues of usability, reliability, performance, support, and design constraints. (See our appendix for a list of these criteria).

Why might you include some or all of these?

- To prove to the customer that every single one of the features agreed to is being implemented, or that every one of the requirements statements is being acted upon.
- To lay the basis for acceptance tests, where the user verifies that in fact the system does what the requirements demand.
- To provide traceability. (A database does a better job of this, but sometimes you have to show the traces in a regular document.)
- To include requirements that are related to the use case, but not apparent in the steps.

What do you call this section?

Features: If you just include features, and no requirements based on them.

Change Requests: If they really are requests for changes.

Special Requirements: This is a weird term, because people sometimes throw in regular functional requirements, along with constraints, while calling this section "special" because, after all, they have already laid out the functional requirements in the steps.

Requirements: This is also a weird term, because a use case is itself thought of as a set of functional requirements, and certainly the system responses within the flows constitute individual functional requirements.

You can see why a lot of people leave this section out.

6. State the Preconditions.

Preconditions characterize the state that the **system** must be in before the use case can start.

A precondition is expressed as a flat statement of fact.

Examples:

- The user is logged into the system.
- The user has a PowerPoint file open.
- The file contains at least one slide.

A precondition is not:

- Something that might happen before, or might not.
- Something that triggers the action (an actor or an external event triggers the action at the beginning of the use case).
- A statement about something that **should** be true, or **might** be true. Just use the present tense. You are describing the actual situation that **must** be in place before the use case begins.

What they may include:

- What must have happened before the user can initiate the use case—and what state the system is in at that moment.
- What data should appear on the screen when the user arrives there.
- Who has access to the actions described in the use case.
- What the developers have to prepare when a person arrives at a form, a page, or a dialog. (For example, the actor's name appears at the top of the screen, with a welcome statement).
- A set of circumstances that must be true for the use case to work. (For example, the user is already an approved vendor, and the price list is already available for display, if requested.)

Why are preconditions helpful?

They tell developers what the circumstances are, at the start of the use case.

They dictate some of the preparations that the developers must make, before the actor can begin.

They reduce the amount of validation: You do not have to test that, say, the Quote System is available at each step, because, by definition, it has to be available before you can begin.

> For example: It is better to say as a precondition, "The user is logged in," than to put that as your first step. It is a prerequisite to doing the use case, but it is not really a step in the use case.

Examples of good preconditions

For a use case on charging with a credit card:

> The Store Customer possesses a valid credit card.
>
> The network connection to the Credit Card System is active.

For a use case on withdrawing cash from an ATM

> The Customer possesses a valid bank card.
>
> The network connection to the Bank System is active.
>
> The system has cash to dispense.
>
> The option Cash Withdrawal is available.

Examples of bad preconditions

For a use case called *Make a Withdrawal*: The withdrawal function works normally.

> What's wrong with this?
>
> It is saying that the functionality you are about to describe already works perfectly. But you may have alternate flows coming up that describe when things go wrong.
>
> Moral: Do not announce that the functionality you are about to describe is working well.

For a use case called *Delete a File*: The file is deleted.

> What's wrong with this?
>
> It announces the result of the whole use case, and says, well, before you can delete a file, it must already be deleted.
>
> Moral: This is a post condition, not a precondition.

7. List all the Scenarios you will cover.

A Scenario is one of the ways that the action can go. For example, the fundamental set of steps in the use case, known as the Basic Flow, forms what's known as the Happy Day scenario, because all the steps flow well, and the user walks away happy.

> We would list the Happy Day scenario first, in this way: Register for Course: Basic Flow.

But perhaps the connection to the database goes down, and the user is unable to complete step 4. Because we are following some of the steps in the Basic Flow, before the crash, that scenario would be:

> Failure to connect to database: Basic Flow, Database Down.

Or the user decides to quit after step 3.

> That scenario would be: User quits: Basic Flow, Quit.

Each is a different scenario.

A scenario has two parts.

Each scenario has a **name**, such as Host Link Down.

Each scenario points to one or more **flows** (the flows that give the actual steps of the scenario—usually the Basic Flow plus one or two alternative flows).

> Failure to connect to host: Basic Flow, Host Link Down

The most important scenario describes the Happy Day—when each step is successful, and the sequence of steps leads you to the goal of the whole use case.

> Example: Get Quote: Basic Flow.

Other scenarios describe the way that sequence is modified by variations, oddball situations, and possible errors. Examples:

> Quit before closing registration: Basic Flow, Quit.
>
> Attempt to close registration too early: Basic Flow, Registration Still in Progress
>
> Billing system host link down: Basic Flow, Billing System Unavailable

To discover alternative scenarios, ask:

- Where do options appear?

- What odd cases crop up?
- What are the variations on the basic flow?
- What can go wrong?
- What might not happen?
- What kind of resources can be blocked?

A scenario does **not** contain:

- A lot of text.
- Any actual names, dates, data, menu items.
- Any specifics about what the user will see on the screen (the user interface) or ways that the user will interact with the user interface (clicking a mouse, dragging across text, hovering over an item, tapping to enlarge).
- A description of any other goals that the user might have. Those would end up in **separate use cases**.

    Example: If you are writing a use case about applying a style to selected text, you would not add a scenario about how to modify a style, or how to create a new style.

Scenarios help because…

- Each scenario describes what the user does, and how the system responds, on the way to a goal that the user cares about, so the scenario helps stakeholders and the team discuss what the system will actually do.
- Scenarios help developers imagine how the system will really be used.
- Each scenario suggests one or more test cases.
- A complete use case represents all the possible sequences that might happen until the resulting value is achieved, or until the system terminates the attempt.

A scenario names a flow that involves a particular sequence of steps. But the scenario itself does not usually hold the steps. The flows will do that.

The team often plans each iteration around some of the use cases' scenarios.

The team usually wants to address the more architecturally significant scenarios first. These scenarios:

- Focus on functionality that is central to the project.
- Cover a lot of the architecture.
- Exercise a lot of architectural elements or interfaces.
- Stress a specific, delicate point of the architecture.
- Involve high risk.

Deciding what to work on next, the team tends to pick ...

- Scenarios that trace back to high-priority stakeholder requests and features.
- Scenarios that represent the main use of the system (80:20 rule).
- Features that earn an incremental payment.
- Features that are a key differentiator from major competitors.

8. Build the Basic Flow.

The basic flow describes the Happy Day, step by step! It is successful. At the end, the user has attained the goal.

- Each step contains two parts: the actor does something in the system, and the system responds.
- At the end of the flow, the actor achieves the goal of the use case.

We often have a column for the step number, then two other columns.

- In the first column, we give the number of the step. (You may also summarize the action, but that tends to be redundant, because the next column says what action the user takes).
- In the next column, we say what the actor does in the system. Each user action pokes the system. Essentially, each user action interacts with the system in some way, goading the system into a response. (Hence, waiting for a call is not a user action in this sense, because the system has no way of knowing that you are anticipating a call).
- In the last column, we say what the system does. (Basically, these responses correspond to one or more statements of functional requirements—what the user wants the system to do).

In each step, the actor does something, and gets a system response. (Round trip). Example:

Step	User action	System response
5	The user chooses to pay the bill.	The system displays three options: Pay the minimum, pay the current statement in full, pay the current balance.
6	The user chooses to pay the minimum.	The system checks with the Billing System, fetches the minimum payment due, and displays that amount in the box with a label that says how much the customer will be paying. It also displays the option to Pay Now.

Notice that you are describing a series of interactions.

- The user does something. The system responds.
- You proceed in chronological order, left to right, top to bottom.
- As in a procedure, you are moving forward moment by moment.

Include all key actions and responses. Don't summarize vaguely.

Do not leave out part of the system response, and then act as if the user has already seen that. For example, you must mention all the options that the system displays, including the one that the user is about to use in the next step. In this way you tell the programmers what to build. And you lay the basis for the user being able to use the option in the next step.

Make sure you include everything that the system does in response, **before** the user takes advantage of the new form, the message, the picture, or whatever. Do not assume that we understand what the system has done.

Label columns, for clarity.

In general, I have found that the column style makes it easy for stakeholders and developers to focus on discrete actions: what the user does, and then, what the system does in response.

Example:

2.1 Basic Flow

Step	User action	System response
1.	The customer enters the Welcome page.	The system asks for User ID and Password.
2.	The customer enters the user ID and password, and chooses to submit.	The system confirms that the user is on the approved list, and welcomes the user.

Go in order.

First the user does something, then the system responds.

Bad example

The user opens the drawing tool.	The system opens the drawing tool.

That's the same action, twice. First say what the user does to provoke the system, then say what the system does.

Better:

The user chooses the drawing tool.	The system opens the drawing area and displays the preset shapes for the rectangle, circle, and line.

Bad example

The user accesses the file.	The system opens the file.

Write a Use Case

Accesses: this word is ambiguous. Do you mean that the user has located the file in the file system? Or do you mean that the user has opened up the file? If so, what is the system response? Here you have the system responding by opening up the file. But how can it do that, if the user has already opened the file?

Better:

| The user selects the file and chooses to open it. | The system opens the file. |

Bad example

At the welcome screen, the user inserts a valid bank card in the ATM.	The system displays three options: Withdraw $300, Make Deposit, Other.
The user enters a valid username and password and clicks Submit.	The system prepares 15 $20 bills, and requests that the user retrieve the bank card.
The user chooses Withdraw $300.	The system dispenses the cash, and asks if the user wants to do another transaction.
The user retrieves the bank card.	The system reverts to the Welcome screen.

What's wrong here?

The actions do not proceed continuously from left to right, top to bottom.

- A key system action has been left out: the request for login before the system offers any options.

- Despite the fact that the system does not request login, the user does that, instead of choosing an option.

- The system prepares the cash before the user requests it.

- The user never answers the question of another transaction. The system just assumes No.

- The use case shows the system options **after** the user has already chosen an option.

Better:

At the welcome screen, the user inserts a valid bank card in the ATM.	The system displays the request for a username and password.
The user enters a valid username and password and clicks Submit.	The system displays three options: Withdraw $300, Make Deposit, Other.
The user chooses Withdraw $300.	The system prepares 15 $20 bills, and requests that the user retrieve the bank card.
The user retrieves the bank card.	The system dispenses the cash, and asks if the user wants to do another transaction.
The user chooses No.	The system reverts to the Welcome screen.

Be precise when describing what the user does.

Bad example

The user selects a paragraph to make italic.	The system makes the text in the paragraph italic.

What's wrong?

> The user just selected the text. The user did not say, "Make this italic." So the system had no business going ahead and making it italic.

> Moral: Make sure that you include every necessary user action leading to the goal. (Not every option. Just every action that leads to the goal).

Better:

The user selects a paragraph to make italic, and chooses to make it italic.	The system makes the text in the paragraph italic.

Write a Use Case

Bad example

| The user issues a command. | The system displays the image in sepia, with the options to accept the change, or cancel. |

What's wrong?

>We do not know what the user asked the system to do. But the system had an intuitive hit and guessed that the user wanted the image transformed into sepia.

Better:

| The user chooses to make the image Sepia. | The system displays the image in sepia, with the options to accept the change, or cancel. |

Include all system actions that the user needs.

If the user is going to have to use an option, then the system must first display that option.

Bad example

The user chooses to rotate the selected object	The system displays options.
The user chooses to rotate the selected object 90 degrees clockwise	The system rotates the object 90 degrees clockwise, leaving the selection handles active.

What's wrong?

>We never hear what options we ought to offer in the first step. And therefore the system has never offered the option of rotating the object 90 degrees clockwise. So the user really cannot do that.
>
>Moral: Include all the options, so that the user can perform the next step...and the programmers know what items to create. If you want to display a record, tell us what fields are on it, so the programmers can build it.

Better:

| The user chooses to rotate the selected object | The system displays the options to rotate 90 degrees clockwise, to rotate 90 degrees counter |

96

		clockwise, to flip horizontally, and to flip vertically.
	The user chooses to rotate the selected object 90 degrees clockwise	The system rotates the object 90 degrees clockwise, leaving the selection handles active.

Bad example

1.	The user logs into the system.	The system detects an incoming signal from the satellite's status-check system.
2.	The user listens for alerts.	The system notifies the user of the signal, and offers the user an option to monitor the satellite status.

What's wrong?

The first user action does not drive the system response. It would be better to just set a precondition that the user is logged in, and then have the system detecting the signal be a trigger, all by itself, in the first row.

And having the user sit around and listen is NOT an action that provokes a response from the system.

It would make more sense to have the system notify the user, as part of the initial trigger.

Better:

Precondition: The user is logged in.

1. (Trigger)		The system detects an incoming signal from the satellite's status-check system. The system notifies the user of the signal, and offers the user an option to monitor the satellite status.
2.	The user chooses to monitor the satellite status.	The system displays the streaming signal in wave form, along with the options to adjust the interval, and to compare to a baseline recording.

Special situation: Triggering the events

The user does not always start the use case.

Sometimes the system does something that provokes the user, forces the user to react. For example, when a call comes in, the phone rings and vibrates. That trigger appears in the first row, in the column for system actions: but there is no user action **before** this (because the user does not know a call is coming in). Hence, in that first row, we leave the User Action cell blank.

Only after the phone announces the call does the user take action—and we put that action into the next row.

In the first row, if the system alerts the user, triggering an action, then the User Action column can be blank.

1. (Trigger)		The system detects an incoming call, and alerts the user. The system displays options to answer the call, send it directly to voicemail, or respond with a text message.
2.	The user chooses to answer the call.	The system enables the connection, so that the user can hear the caller, and vice versa.

When the phone vibrates and rings to indicate an incoming call, that triggers the user action.

Mantra: A user action must always be an action that the system perceives. Nothing else counts. Psychic moments are not user actions.

9. Consider Subflows.

But only if you are working on a big complicated system.

Tip: Usually, you do **not** need subflows.

A subflow is a like a subroutine, a set of one or more steps that **must** be performed every time the use case runs. It is pulled out simply to clarify the flow; and quite often, we use the same subflow in several different use cases, such as logging in, or quitting the application.

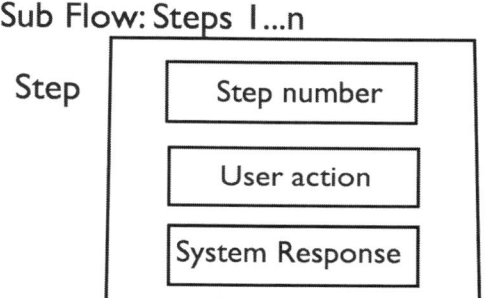

If the flow becomes too complicated, factor out some part of the flow, as an internal include, that is, a subflow.

How?

1. Create a section for subflows right after the Basic Flow, before Alternative Flows.
2. Label each subflow with a prefix such as S.
3. Name the subflow.
4. Call the subflow in the Basic Flow.
5. Do not mention the subflow in a scenario, because it is really just a step in the Basic Flow.

Why invent a subflow?

> You can repeat the same set of steps over and over, without cluttering up the Basic Flow.
>
> Because the subflow is called by the Basic Flow, it always returns to the flow at the next line (like a subroutine call). In the following example, the subflow is called in step 3, and returns control to the basic flow in step 4).

Example
: Basic Flow

1. Log on.
2. Select Create a Schedule.
3. Obtain Course Information.

    Perform Subflow S1: Obtain Course Information.

4. Select Courses.
5. Submit Schedule.
6. Accept Completed Schedule.

: Subflows

S1: Obtain Course Information

The student requests a list of course offerings. The student can search the list by department, professor or topic to obtain the course information. The system retrieves a list of available courses from the Course Catalog System and displays the list to the student.

Against subflows

We generally create a subflow only on big projects. When we have dozens of use cases, or a hundred, we may notice that we are writing the same three or four steps over and over. To avoid that, we may create a subflow called Stuff, and invoke it each time, to avoid writing it over and over.

So a subflow is a convenience....and a dubious one at that. After all, it makes those steps seem "invisible" to the casual reader.

Plus, the folks representing the users tend to forget what the heck Stuff involves.

So the rule of thumb is: If you have a subflow, it must be performed every time you do the basic flow. But most people find subflows more trouble than they are worth. Better to just write the darn steps over and over, so that each use case has all its steps right there.

10. List Alternative Flows.

These alternative flows reflect exceptions, (the database is not available), options (the user adds another course), and errors (the user enters 1900 as the year).

(These are very brief; usually just a statement of what goes wrong, and the system response).

> Example
>
> Alt3: Cancel the Display Function: In Step 5, when the system asks the user to confirm or cancel the function, the user chooses Cancel. The system cancels the function and returns to the home screen. The use case ends.

What might be alternative flows?

- Variations of the Happy Day.
- Exceptions
- Errors
- IF-THEN-ELSE conditions
- Repeated behavior

Alternative flows are detours.

- Regular variants: Handle freshman enrolments differently
- Odd cases: Handle registration for more than 25 credit hours differently
- Exceptions (errors): Invalid student ID

Alternative flows appear in their own separate section.

They appear after the Basic Flow.

Each has a number (usually A1…An) and a name.

Key distinction: An alternative flow intrudes into the Basic Flow like an error message, whereas a subflow is **always** called from the Basic Flow.

An alternative flow is NOT:

- Another way of doing something like what this use case covers. For example, if the product offers three different form factors, each designed for viewing something different (classic movies, say, sports, and regular TV), then each of those would represent a different goal for the user, and each would become its own use case. We would not write a use case about setting the TV for watching sports, and handle the other two form factors as mere alternative flows.

- Another interesting use case that has some vague connection with this one. (Ask yourself: Is this proposed alternative flow really related to the **goal** of this use case?)

- Another use case that deals with the same objects or actions, such as files, or selecting text, but with a different goal: deleting, say, where your use case is about changing.

How to come up with alternative flows

If your use case is about applying a style to selected text, a reasonable alternative flow would be:

User quits file before applying style: Basic Flow, Quit.

Not good would be:

- User modifies a style.
- User deletes a style.
- User creates headings.
- User logs in.

None of these are integral to the basic flow leading the user to apply a style. That flow is very simple.

1. User selects text.
2. User chooses to view styles.
3. User chooses style to apply to text.

But if the user quits before applying the style, that would break the basic flow. So it counts as an alternative flow.

Within your alternative flow, describe:

- Where in the Basic Flow this could happen. (Location, a step #)
- When it could happen. (Condition).
- What the user does (Action)
- What the system does. (System response)

102

- Where the Basic Flow resumes (Resume Location). Or where it stops: The use case ends.

Examples

A3 Request Additional Quotes

> In Step 3, Customer Gets Quote, in the Basic Flow, the customer chooses to get additional quotes, gets the quotes, and the use case continues at Step 3.

A4 Quit

> In any step, the customer decides to quit, and the use case ends.

A5 Unknown Trading Symbol

> In Step 3, Customer Gets Quote, in the Basic Flow, if the system cannot recognize the trading symbol, the system notifies the customer that the trading symbol is not recognizable, and asks the customer to re-enter it or correct it. The use case continues at the beginning of Step 3.

Instead of putting conditions (IF...THEN...ELSE) into your basic flow, use alternative flows.

Why? The conditionals are hard to test accurately.

Move those out of the basic flow, and put them into alternative flows.

Inline version:

> IF the system is unable to communicate with the Quote System THEN the system informs the customer and the use case ends. ELSE the system presents the corresponding Quote Display. ENDIF.

Revised as an alternative flow:

> A6: In Step 3, Customer Gets Quote, in the Basic Flow, if the system is unable to communicate with the Quote System, the system informs the customer, and the use case ends.

If you might have repetitions of some or all steps, put the repetition into an alternate flow.

Alternate flow:

> A7: In Step 3, Customer Gets Quote, in the Basic Flow, if the customer wants another quote, the system supplies that as often as wanted, until the customer moves to the next step or logs off.

11. Identify Extension Points. (Optional)

We have seen two ways to break out of the flow and include additional behavior—by naming a subflow or alternative flow within the steps.

Another way is to mark certain spots as Extension Points, giving each one a name (usually boldfaced within curly brackets). Then, at the beginning of your subflow or alternative flow, you refer to that name as the location where your steps start.

Example

>A few steps in the Basic Flow, with extension points:
>
>>1. The Customer selects Products.
>>
>>**{Display Product Catalog}**
>>
>>2. The Customer selects a Product and enters the number of units.
>>
>>**{Out of Stock}**
>
>Subflow
>
>>S1 Display Product Catalog
>>
>>1. At **{Display Product Catalog}** the system displays the major product categories.
>>
>>2. The Customer chooses a category.
>>
>>3. The system displays the items within that category.
>
>Alternative Flow
>
>>A1 Out of Stock
>>
>>1. At **{Out of Stock}** if the status of the product is Out of Stock, the system informs the customer that the order cannot be fulfilled, and asks if the customer would like to choose an alternate.
>>
>>2. If the customer agrees, the system displays a list of products whose status is Substitute for the original product. The flow resumes.
>>
>>3. If the customer refuses, the system returns the display of the list of products. The flow resumes.
>
>Extension Points
>
>>**{Display Product Catalog}**
>>
>>**{Out of Stock}**

The Extension Points section simply lists the extension points.

> In this example, the Subflow called Display Product Catalog is called after step 1, and the Alternative Flow called Out of Stock is called after 2, if the condition is met (if the product has the status of Out of Stock).

If you insert Extension Points into the steps, you can list them in this section. The extending behavior can be:

- Subflow: behavior that must be included every time the use case runs.
- Alternative Flow: behavior that may optionally extend the flow

Good news: Most people do not rely on extension points. In general, we go with alternate flows, without inserting any extension points.

12. Describe Post Conditions.

Post conditions describe the state of the **system** at the end of the use case.

Each post condition is something that the team can **test**, to make sure it is true. If it is true after doing the use case, then the code meets the requirements.

So don't add irrelevant stuff such as, "And the program remains operational," or "And the project team is extremely happy."

Just focus on an **observable result** of the basic flow. If the use case is Delete a File, then the post condition is: The file is deleted.

Often the post condition is something like:

- The font is changed to the new style.
- The file is saved.
- The map appears in outline.

A post condition is something that is **guaranteed** to be true when the use case is complete.

- We ignore alternative flows were followed. In fact, we do not mention any end results from alternative flows. Just the Happy Day.
- Usually there is just one post condition, and it describes the condition at the end of the basic flow of the use case.

Examples of post conditions

In a use case called Authenticate Customer:

> The Customer has been authorized to use the card.

In a use case called Withdraw Cash:

> The ATM has returned the card and dispensed the cash to the Customer, and the withdrawal is registered on the Customer's account.

Example of a bad post condition

At the end of a use case called Change the Shipping Address:

> If the user has completed all the fields, and clicked Change, as required, the system stores the new shipping address. If the user got the ZIP code wrong, the system posts an error message, and waits until the customer fixes the value. If the user exits the page

5. Creating a use case

before completing the address change, the system does not change the original shipping address.

What's wrong?

The post condition has too many doubts. It is not confident that the user completed the steps successfully. It wonders if the user may have wandered into the various alternative flows, and ended the use case before it reached success, so it tells us the post conditions for those too.

And it leaves out a key part of the system state at the end of the basic flow: the fact that the new shipping address appears on the checkout page.

Better:

The system has stored the new shipping address, and returned the user to the checkout page, which shows the new shipping address.

13. Add an Activity Diagram. (Optional)

You may want to include an activity diagram if the flows are complicated—for instance, you have several subflows, and alternative flows, and maybe even a few different actors.

The **activity diagram** models the flow of control from action to action within the use case.

An **activity** involves one or more actions, each of which may change the state of the system, or send messages.

- The whole diagram shows an entire use case, including the basic flow, and any subflows or alternative flows.
- Individual actions correspond to steps, subflows, or alternative flows.

Generally, an activity diagram shows how the business operates—the **workflow**.

Building the diagram

The flow starts at one spot, represented by an empty circle.

Actions appear in rounded boxes.

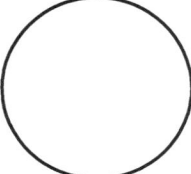

Typical actions:

- Call another operation.
- Send a signal.
- Send a message.
- Create an object.
- Delete an object.
- Perform a calculation.

5. Creating a use case

The flow of control is indicated by arrows.

A decision, or branch, is indicated by a diamond.

> The arrows from the diamond indicate alternate answers to the question.

When two flows of control join, you use a synchronization bar, to indicate that from that moment on, a single action takes over.

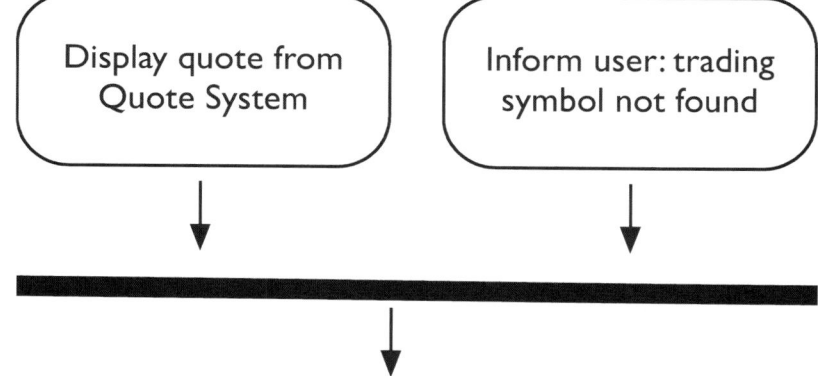

When one flow breaks into two forks, you use the same kind of bar.

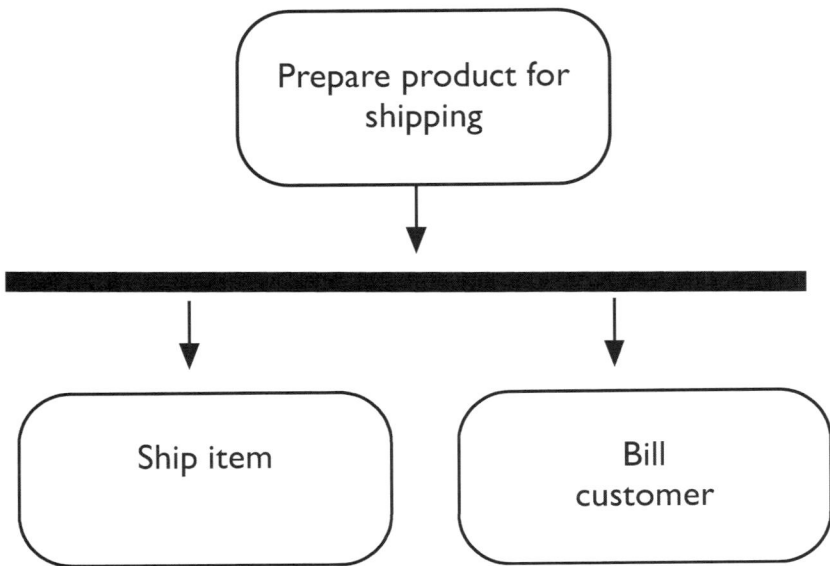

To indicate who does what, arrange the actions in swimlanes. Each swimlane shows the actions that a particular actor performs.

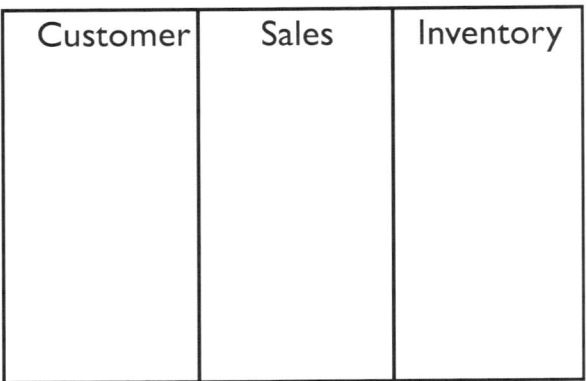

The flow ends at one or more spots, indicated by bull's eyes.

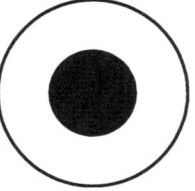

5. Creating a use case

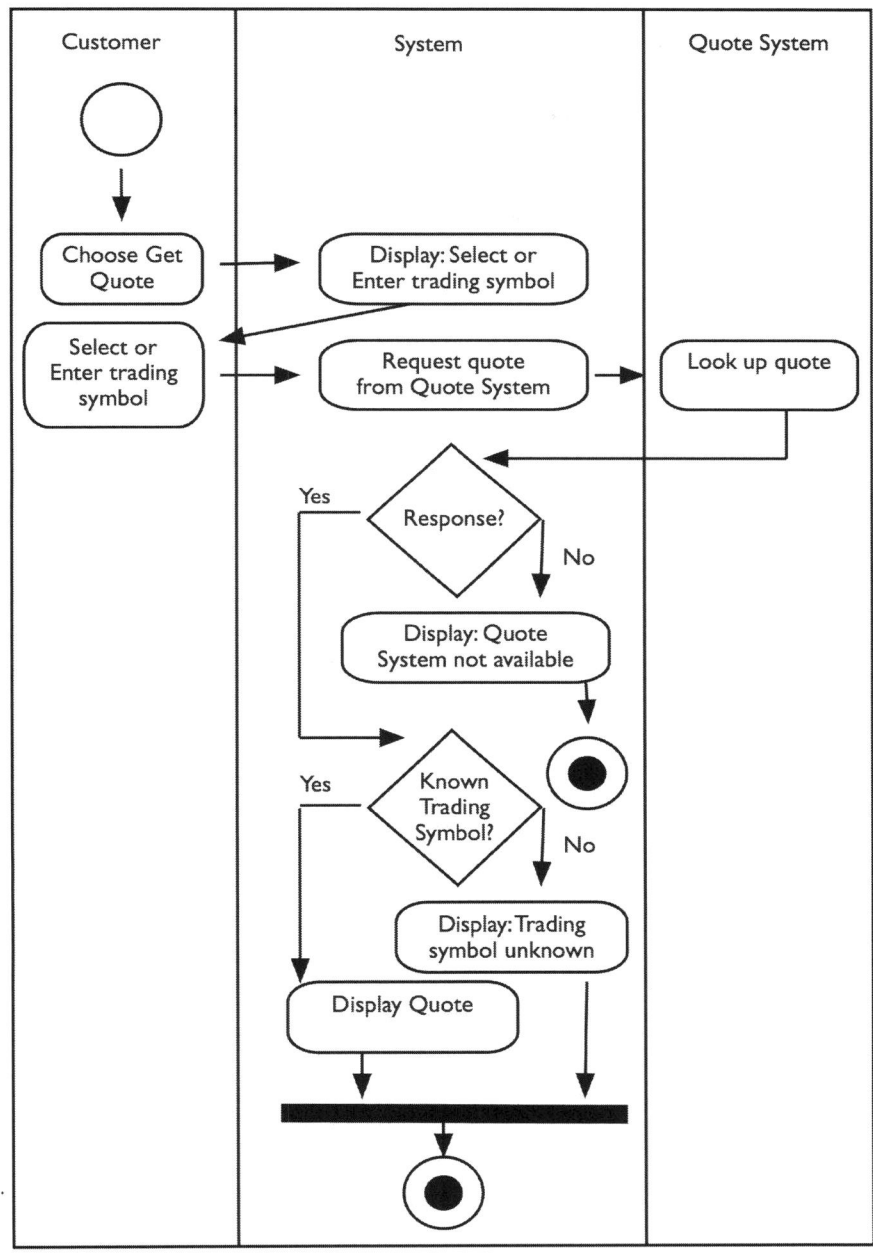

111

Tips on writing use cases

Follow a standard organization, even if it is not the one I outline here.

Make the use case big enough to contain an unambiguous description of the way the system should behave.

Avoid describing the user interface.

> Why?
> - You don't want to anticipate or constrain the actual design.
> - You can't really describe visual elements very accurately. (Better to show samples, during the Design and Analysis Phase).
> - Your system may have to work in different environments, on different platforms, with different interfaces (different cellphones, desktop computers).

Avoid terms that suggest or define the user interface, such as:

- Click.
- Drag.
- Drop.
- Open.
- Close.
- Button.
- Field.
- Menu.
- Window.

Prefer generic actions:

- Start.
- Submit.
- Choose.
- Specify.
- Select.

Consider moving the full details of a form to the glossary.

> Why?
>
>> The details of the fields can get distracting when they are included in the step.
>
> Example:
>
>> Use Case:
>>
>>> The system prompts the customer to enter Customer Details.
>>> The Customer enters the **Customer Details**.
>>> The Customer chooses to create an account.
>>
>> Glossary
>>
>>> **Customer Details**: Information that identifies the customer, and provides contact information. The information consists of: Last Name, First Name, Middle Initial Honorific, Street Address 1, Street Address 2, City, State, ZIP, and daytime phone number.

Include every action that the system must take.

> Don't wave your hand and say something vague like "The system requests some information."
>
>> What information? We need to know exactly what fields to create in the database, so you have to tell us what categories of information the system ought to ask for.
>
> Work from moment to moment.
>
>> When the system responds, it may do several things before the user can do the next step. Please describe each thing the system does, clearly, separately, **before** you have the user take the next action.
>
>> Example: The system validates the credit card information, displays a confirmation message, and displays a message offering new products.

Only do a use case if it ends up giving value to the actor.

> **Not** worth a use case: Enter Student ID. (The student really does not get much value out of this).
>
> **Not** worth a use case: Log in. (No one dreams of logging in. Logging in may be a step, or even a precondition, but it is never a use case),

Recognize that every group has its own style.

We focus on columns for user actions and system response, to make sure that we distinguish those, and describe the system responses fully. But there are other ways to describe the interactions. For example, here are two additional ways to label steps:

The Rational Unified Process Style

2.1 Basic Flow

1. Customer Logs On.

   The trading customer logs on. The system asks for the user ID and password. The customer provides that information. The system presents a list of available functions.

....

2.2 Alternative Flows

   2.2.1 Unidentified Trading Customer

   In Step 1, Customer Logs On, in the Basic Flow, the system determines that the user ID and password combination is invalid, and an error message is displayed.

Tag style

2.1 Basic Flow

   {Trading Customer Logs on}

   1. Customer Logs On.

....

2.2 Alternative Flows

   2.2.1 Unidentified Trading Customer

   In {Trading Customer logs on} Customer Logs on, in the Basic Flow, the system determines that the user ID and password combination is invalid, and an error message is displayed.

Usability.gov styles

Usability.gov offers simple, middleweight, and heavyweight examples.

Simple Laundry Use Case

Use Case 1	Do laundry
Actor	Housekeeper
Basic Flow	On Wednesdays the housekeeper reports to the laundry room. She <u>sorts the laundry</u> that is there. Then she <u>washes each load</u>. She <u>dries each load</u>. She <u>folds the items</u> that need folding. She <u>irons</u> and <u>hangs</u> the items that are wrinkled. She throws away any laundry item that is irrevocably shrunken, soiled or scorched.

Middleweight Laundry Use Case

Use Case 1	Do laundry
Actor	Housekeeper
Basic Flow	On Wednesdays the housekeeper reports to the laundry room. She <u>sorts the laundry</u> that is there. Then she <u>washes each load</u>. She <u>dries each load</u>. She <u>folds the items</u> that need folding. She throws away any laundry item that is irrevocably shrunken, soiled or scorched.
Alternative Flow 1	If she notices that something is wrinkled, she irons it and then hangs it on a hanger.
Alternative Flow 2	If she notices that something is still dirty, she rewashes it.
Alternative Flow 3	If she notices that something shrank, she throws it out.

Heavyweight Laundry Use Case

Use Case 1	Do laundry
Actor	Housekeeper
Use Case Overview	It is Wednesday and there is laundry in the laundry room. The housekeeper sorts it, then proceeds to launder each load. She folds the dry laundry as she removes it from the dryer. She irons those items that need ironing.
Subject Area	Domestics
Actor(s)	The housekeeper
Trigger	Dirty laundry is transported to the laundry room on Wednesday.
Precondition 1	It is Wednesday.

Write a Use Case

Precondition 2		There is laundry in the laundry room.
Flows		
Basic Flow		Do laundry
Description		This scenario describes the situation where only sorting, washing and folding are required. This is the main success scenario.
	1	Housekeeper sorts laundry items.
	2	Housekeeper washes each load.
	3	Housekeeper dries each load.
	4	Housekeeper verifies that laundry item does not need ironing, is clean and not shrunken.
	5	Housekeeper verifies that laundry item is foldable.
	6	Housekeeper folds laundry item.
	7	Housekeeper does this until there are no more laundry items to fold.
Termination outcome		Laundry is clean and folded.
Alternative Flow 4a		Laundry item needs ironing.
Description		This scenario describes the situation where one or more items need ironing before or in lieu of folding.
	4a1	Housekeeper verifies that the laundry item needs ironing and is clean and not shrunken.
	4a2	Housekeeper irons the laundry item.
	4a3	Housekeeper puts laundry item on a hanger.
Termination outcome		Laundry that needs ironing is ironed and hung up.
Alternative flow 4b		Laundry item is dirty.
Description		This scenario describes the situation where the laundry item did not get clean the first time through the wash.
	4b1	Housekeeper verifies that the laundry item is not clean.
	4b2	Housekeeper rewashes the laundry item.
Termination outcome		Dirty laundry is rewashed.
Alternative flow 4c		Laundry item shrank.
Description		This scenario describes the situation where the laundry item shrank.
	4c1	Housekeeper verifies that the laundry item shrank.
	4c2	Housekeeper disposes of laundry item.
Termination outcome		Laundry item no longer exists.

Alternative flow 5a	Laundry item needs hanger.
Description	This scenario describes the situation where the laundry item needs to be hung instead of folded.
5a1	Housekeeper verifies that laundry item needs hanging.
5a2	Housekeeper puts laundry item on a hanger.
Termination outcome	Laundry that needs hanging is hung up.
Post conditions	All laundry clean and folded or hung up.
Business Rules	1. Laundry can only be done on Wednesdays. 2. All ironed laundry items get hung on hangers. 3. Any laundry item that is irrevocably soiled, shrunken, scorched, etc., gets thrown out.

Source: https://www.usability.gov/how-to-and-tools/methods/use-cases.html

Form Approved OMB# 0990-0379 Exp. Date 9/30/2020

In this book, then, I describe a fairly middle-of-the-road method for creating use cases. But your mileage will vary.

Sample: From needs to a use case

To give you an idea of the way we move from needs to a use case, here are samples along the way. We start with selected excerpts from the raw material.

Interviews

We have to bring the students into the gym, where we have tables set up with information, you know. We have professors sitting there to tell the students about the courses.

Then the students come over to us, to register. They fill out a form, and give it to us, and we check which courses are free, and we try to remember to make sure that the times don't conflict, and then we look up the prerequisites in the catalog, but of course, you have to look in different places for the prerequisites, and not every department does those the same way, so it can take half an hour, just to register a student in one class.

And then, you know, we do seniors on the first day, and juniors the next, and so on…so by the time the freshmen come in, most courses are oversubscribed, and we have to say, sorry, you can only take one of these giant 101 courses, because all the upper level courses have been grabbed.

I don't think we should keep that kind of priority in the new system, if you ask me. It should be first come first serve. But that's just my opinion. (Registrar's clerk).

It's a zoo. It reminds me of lining up at 4 a.m. to get into the mall stores on the day after Thanksgiving. But once you get in, you have to wait forever, and if you are not first in line, you may not get the courses you want. Why can't we do this online, anyway? (Student).

We need to be able to have automatic checks of prerequisites, because the manual process takes too long and it is full of errors. (Registrar).

Requests (verbatim)

The system shall prevent conflicts between courses (courses at the same time, for example).

The system shall verify that the student really is enrolled in the university, and has a valid ID and password. If not, the student does not get to register for courses.

5. Creating a use case

The system needs to go look up course information in our Course Catalog system, which runs on SQL Server.

The screen must have a big red Quit button, so that students can quit the program at any time.

If someone quits, we want to save the schedule as it stands.

When someone quits, and we are going to save the schedule as it stands, we must indicate which courses the student has successfully enrolled in, and which ones are just possibilities, or items on a wish list.

The student must not be allowed to sign up for more than six courses.

The student must be able to see the course description from the Course Catalog System.

If the Course Catalog system is not available, we have to put a message saying, "The Course Catalog System is not currently available. Please check back in a few hours. Or call Extension 767."

I wrote one course description in May for the catalog, but for the registration shindig, I had to write another, because the catalog had not been printed, and they had no access to the electronic version. I would like to write it once, and have it available in the online catalog, and also whenever they are signing up for courses.

Stakeholder Needs (excerpts from the Vision document)

Registrar's Needs

- The Registrar needs complete accuracy in checking prerequisites, so that students are not accidentally enrolled in a class they should not be taking.
- The Registrar wants to make sure that students cannot accidentally sign up for two classes that meet at the same time.
- The Registrar wants to make sure that once a class has filled, no one else can sign up for it.
- Also, if a class does not meet its minimum quota, they need to be able to cancel it, and keep other students from signing up from then on.
- The Registrar needs to be able to get an onscreen or printed report of enrolments by class, department, and semester.

Registrar's Staff

- Everyone wants to speed up the process of registering for classes, by automating it.

- To help students, the staff needs to be able to see the student's current schedule. Some kind of override may be necessary, eventually.

- Courses vary from one semester to another, and from campus to campus, so we need students to tell us which semester they are enrolling for, and where, and in what department.

Students

- The students want to be able to register for courses online.

- The students want the process to be fast.

- The students want to get confirmation that they have enrolled in the classes that they think they have signed up for.

Faculty

- The faculty members want to make sure that students have the right prerequisites for upper-level courses, before they are allowed to enroll.

- The faculty wants to write course descriptions once, and have the same description used in the catalog and during registration.

- The faculty wants to keep classes open until the last possible moment, so students can fill those classes...but once a class is closed for lack of enrolment, no more students should be allowed to sign up.

- The faculty wants the system to prevent students from enrolling in a class that is already full.

Features (Excerpts from the Vision document)
Communication with the Course Catalog System
- The system will display course descriptions from the Course Catalog System.
- If the Course Catalog System is not available, the system will explain that to the student.
- Courses will be filtered by semester, campus, and department.

Goals
- The system will automate the process of signing up for courses.
- The system will check the proposed schedule quickly.

Following the Rules
- The system will only give access to students who appear on the List of Enrolled Students.
- The system will prevent students from accidentally signing up for two courses that meet at the same time.
- The system will make sure students have the prerequisites for a course.
- The system will make sure students can't sign up for a class that has been canceled or filled.
- The system will prevent students from enrolling before registration begins or after registration closes.

Exceptions
- If a student quits in the middle of signing up for courses, the system will preserve the schedule so far, showing which courses are enrolled, and which are just candidates for possible enrolment.
- If a student's ID cannot be validated, the system will prevent that student from registering for any classes.

Reports
- The system shall allow administrators to pull reports on class enrolments by class, department, or semester.
- The system will allow staff to pull up an individual student's schedule.

Excerpt from the use-case model

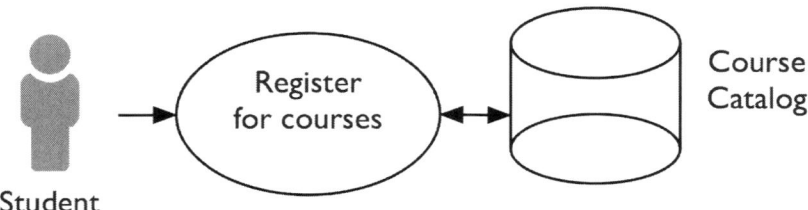

Excerpts from the list of functional requirements

#	Group	Requirement
	Access	
1		The system must confirm the User ID and Password of a student by comparing those to the List of Enrolled Students.
2		If a student's User ID and Password do not match any entry in the List of Enrolled Students, the system must display a message refusing access.
3		If a student's User ID and Password do match an entry in the List of Enrolled Students, the system must check the day's date against the date for Beginning Registration.
4		If a student signs in before the date for Beginning Registration, the system must refuse to allow the student to register.
5		If a student signs in after the date for Closing Registration, the system must refuse to allow the student to register.
6		If the day's date falls between the Beginning Registration date, and the date for Closing Registration, and if the student appears in the List of Enrolled Students, the system must display a page on which the student can register for courses
	Options	
7		The system must allow the student to quit at any time.

8			If the student chooses to quit before completing registration for one or more courses that were selected, the system must offer to save the schedule.
9			If a student chooses to quit, and OKs saving the schedule, the system must indicate which courses are enrolled.
10			If a student chooses to quit, and OKs saving the schedule, the system must indicate which courses are selected, but not enrolled.
	Course Listings		
11			The system must offer the student the option of creating a schedule.
12			The system must ask the student what campus he or she attends.
13			The system must ask the student what semester he or she is planning to build a schedule for.
14			The system must ask what department the student wants to select courses from.
15			The system must query the Course Catalog System for a list of courses that meet the criteria for campus, semester, and department.
16			When the list of courses is returned by the Course Catalog System, the system must display that list.
17			For each course in the list of courses, the Course Catalog System must return a list of prerequisite courses.
18			The system must allow the student to select up to six courses.
	Checking the schedule		
19			The system must allow the student to submit a proposed schedule of courses for verification.
20			For each course that the student chooses, the system must confirm that the class schedule does not overlap the class schedule of any other course that the student is already enrolled in.

21		For each course that the student chooses, the system must confirm that the student's transcript indicates that the student has passed each of the prerequisite courses.
22		The system must store the list of courses that each student has passed.
23		For each course that the student chooses, the system must confirm that the course does not have a status of Cancelled.
24		For each course that the student chooses, the system must confirm that the course does not have a status of Filled.
25		For each course that the student chooses, if the student has met all prerequisites, and the course is not Cancelled or Filled, the system must enroll the student in that course.
26		When the system enrolls a student in a course, the system must give the student a confirming message.
27		The confirming message for enrolment in a course must include a unique confirmation number.
28		The system must save the student's registration record for each course.
	Reports	
29		The system must allow administrators to pull reports on class enrolments by class, department, or semester.
30		The system must allow staff to pull up an individual student's schedule.

Excerpts from the Glossary

Beginning Registration: The date on which Registration starts, at the start of business.

Cancelled: A course is cancelled by the system if enrollment fails to meet a minimum number by the last week of registration.

Class Days: The days of the week on which the class meets.

Class End Time: The time when the class meeting ends.

Class Meeting Length: The amount of time used by each class meeting, calculated by subtracting the class start time from the class end time.

Class Meeting: A single session of the class.

Class Schedule: A combination of the class days, class start time, and class end time.

Class Start Time: The time when the class meeting begins.

Closing Registration: The date on which Registration stops, at the close of business.

Course Description: Text written by the faculty, stored in the Course Catalog System.

Filled: A course is considered Filled if the number of registration records for that course in that semester reach the maximum enrolment number.

Maximum Enrolment Number: The highest number of students allowed into one course in one semester.

Prerequisites: Courses that the student must have passed before being allowed to take another course.

Registration Record: Data showing that one student has signed up for one seat in one class in one semester on one campus.

Use Case #5: Register for Courses

Brief Description

The student enters the system, and chooses to register for courses. The system allows the student to choose a department, a campus, and a semester. The system then pulls the list of courses from the Course Catalog system. The student picks up to six courses, and completes registration.

Status: Draft

Actors: Student, Course Catalog system

Diagram

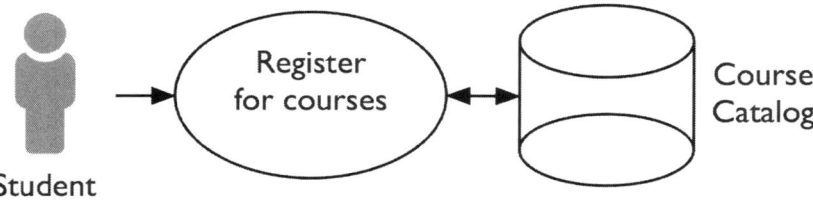

Scenarios (and Alternative Scenarios)

- Register for courses: Basic Flow
- Unidentified student: Basic Flow, Unidentified Student
- Quit before registering: Basic Flow, Quit
- Cannot enroll: Basic Flow, Cannot Enroll.
- Registration closed: Basic Flow, Registration Closed.
- Course Catalog System Unavailable: Basic Flow, Course Catalog System Unavailable

Preconditions

- The system has communication with the Course Catalog System.
- The list of courses for the semester has been created in the Course Catalog System.
- The student has already set up an account. On login, the system confirms that he or she is a currently enrolled student, with no outstanding charges.

Basic Flow		
Step	Student Action	System Response
1. Log On	Student accesses the system's welcome page.	The system asks for identification.
	Student enters a valid User ID and password.	System validates the ID and password, and displays the registration page, with the option to Create a Schedule.
2. Select Create a Schedule	Student chooses Create a Schedule.	The system asks for the campus, semester, and department.
3. Obtain course information.	The student enters the campus, semester, and department.	The system displays a list of course titles, drawn from the Course Catalog System.
4. Select courses.	The student selects a course.	The system adds that to the student's schedule, and offers to display a list of courses for the same department, or another one.
	The student continues to select courses, up to a maximum of six.	
5. Submit schedule	The student submits the schedule.	The system verifies that the courses do

		not overlap or conflict on times. For each course, the system verifies that the student has the prerequisites, that the course has open slots. The system enrolls the student in each course. The system displays the completed schedule, with a confirmation number.
6. Confirm schedule	The student confirms the completed schedule.	The system saves the student's registrations for each course. The use case ends.

Alternative Flows

Unidentified Student

> In Step 1, Log On, if the system discovers that the student ID and password combination is not valid, the system displays an error message. The use case ends.

Quit

> The system allows the student to quit at any time. If the student chooses to quit, the system asks if the student wants to save a partial schedule before quitting. All courses in which the student is already enrolled are marked Enrolled. Any courses that the student selected, but did not enroll in, are marked Selected. If the student approves of saving the schedule, it is saved. The use case ends.

Course Catalog System Unavailable

> In Step 3, Obtain Course Information, in the Basic Flow, if the system is unable to communicate with the Course Catalog System, it displays an error message to the student. The student acknowledges the message. The use case ends.

Cannot Enroll

> In Step 5, Submit Schedule, if the system discovers that a course conflicts with the time of another, or that the student does not have the prerequisites for the course, or that the course has been cancelled, or filled, the system does not enroll the student in the course. A message appears suggesting that the student pick another course. The use case continues at Step 4, Select Courses, in the Basic Flow.

Registration Closed

> In Step 1, Log On, if the student signs in successfully at a time when enrolment has not yet opened, or has already been closed, the system displays a message. The use case ends.

Special Requirements

The system must validate or reject a schedule within one minute of the time that the student submits it.

Extension Points

None.

Post Conditions

At the end of the use case, the student has been enrolled in courses and received a confirmed schedule, and the system saves the registrations.

Checklist for a use case

Use this checklist to confirm that you are writing each element successfully.

ID

The ID for the use case is unique.

The ID follows the conventions set up by the development team.

Name

The name describes the goal of the user.

The name begins with a verb.

The name takes the point of view of the primary actor (a person, not the system).

The name describes something of value to the user.

The name does not focus on something that is more important to the system than to the user, such as logging in.

The name describes the steps of the Basic Flow, and its main result.

Brief Description

You describe each major step that the primary actor takes.

You are brief. (Each step takes a sentence or less).

You do not talk about "the use case," or "the flow."

You resist talking about the system, its wonders, and its many options.

You describe what constitutes success at the end of the basic flow.

If you have significant alternative flows, you mention each one separately after the basic flow.

Status

You use one of a set of agreed-upon terms.

Actors

The Primary Actor appears first.

The name of the Primary Actor is sufficiently abstract to cover all users in that role.

The name of the Primary Actor describes the role, or the class of people for whom the use case is most valuable.

You do not include rare, casual, or occasional users as separate actors.

You do not include anyone as an actor if that person or system does not perform or receive some action in the use case.

You include other systems that must interact with this one—sending data to your system, or receiving data from your system during the basic flow.

The product you are building, known as "the system," does not appear in the list of actors. The system is the product you are building, so the whole use case assumes its existence.

Requirements

You only include this section when the stakeholders need to be able to trace the origins of the use case.

You include any of the following, if stakeholders feel they would shed light on the use case:

- Features
- Functional requirement statements
- Change requests
- Business rules
- Special requirements

You do not include any of these if they are irrelevant to this particular use case. For example, if your use case is Purchase a Product, then you do not include requirements about health benefits for workers, even if they work in the warehouse that will ship the product.

Scenarios

Each scenario has a name.

Each scenario has one or more flows, such as the Basic Flow plus one or two alternative flows.

The first scenario describes the Happy Day. That is the Basic Flow.

Alternative scenarios address variations on the Basic Flow, such as options, errors, failures.

Every scenario deals directly with the user's goal described in the name of the use case.

Each scenario is brief.

Write a Use Case

No scenario contains specifics about the user interface.

Preconditions

Each precondition describes a situation that must be in place before the use case can begin.

Each situation is something that MUST occur before the user can start the use case.

Each precondition is described as a factual statement: This is true.

No *musts*.

No *shoulds*.

You include actions that lead up to the use case, but that do not form part of the use case. Examples: logging in, opening a file. You assume those have been done, by stating them as preconditions. Therefore, these actions do **not** appear in the flows.

The use case cannot start unless each precondition is met.

Basic Flow

The Primary Actor or a trigger event launches the use case.

Each user action provokes a system response.

You include each action that the user performs, moment to moment.

You do not describe the user interface, because that has not been designed yet. Therefore, you do not use words such as *click, drag, drop, open, close, button, field, menu, tab,* or *window*.

Your descriptions of user actions are focused on the action, not the technique: *initiate, start, submit, choose, specify, select*.

If your user must fill in multiple fields on a form, you move the details to a glossary, to make the use case easier to follow.

Each system response makes it possible or necessary for the user to take the next action.

Each system response includes all the actions that the system performs before the next user action.

One system response may include multiple actions, such as validating user information and displaying a confirmation screen.

If you have your system sending information to another system, that other system becomes an actor, and in the next row, takes the action of responding to your own system.

A user action includes as many actions as take place before the next time that the system responds.

The steps follow chronological order: that is, first the user acts, then the system responds, and then (in the next row) the user acts again.

The name of the step describes the combination of user action and system response. It is not the same as the user action.

If you are using a table, one step has one or more rows.

You describe the system response from the outside; that is, you do not include algorithms, calculations, code.

At the end of the last system response, you announce that you have reached the end of the use case.

Alternative Flows

Each alternate flow has a number and a name.

Each alternate flow appears in a scenario (above).

Each alternate flow deals directly with the user's goal that forms the use case name, offering a variation on the Basic Flow, an exception, an error situation, an option (if-then-else), or a special repetition.

You do not include a flow that deals with similar objects, but for a different purpose. For example, if your use case deals with applying a style, you do not include an alternative flow about deleting a style.

Each alternate flow identifies where, in the Basic Flow, it could happen.

Each alternate flow identifies the conditions under which this might happen.

Each alternate flow describes what the user does, and how the system responds.

Each alternate flow describes where the Basic Flow resumes (or stops).

Subflows

Your subflow contains actions that **must** be performed every time that the use case runs.

Your subflow acts like a subroutine in a program; that is, it is always called by the main program.

You have excerpted the subflow for a good reason. One good reason: You use these steps in dozens of other use cases, and you want to make sure they are exactly the same in every use case.

Post condition

The post condition describes the state of the system at the end of the use case.

The post condition can be tested by a programmer looking at the system.

The post condition is guaranteed to be true when the use case ends.

Activity Diagram

You only include the activity diagram when your basic flow is so complex that stakeholders could use a visual aid.

You model the flow of control from one action to the next throughout the use case.

The diagram shows the entire use case.

Individual actions correspond to steps, subflows, or alternative flows.

The diagram shows a workflow.

You use conventional symbols for

- Starting and ending points
- Actions
- Flow of control
- Swimlanes

Chapter 6. Creating a test case

Some portion of the product has been developed, and now we want to know if it works.

To find out, the developers run many different kinds of automated tests. But the most important tests, at least for us, as writers, are ones that ask normal users to try out the product, to see if it functions well under their fingers.

- Does it meet the functional requirements?
- Does it do what the use cases said it should do?

In these functional test cases, then, we write very detailed instructions for the test participants to act on, and we describe in great detail what **should** happen after they perform the action.

We write test cases for two audiences.

When creating test cases for functional requirements, we write for:

- The test **participant**, the person who performs the test.
- The **development team members**, who set up the test, watch as it goes on, and fix any bugs that are discovered.

The **test participant** just wants to know what to do, to check that the product works as expected.

- The test participant follows your instructions to the letter.
- The test participant checks to make sure that the system responses are exactly the ones that you predict…the ones that the requirements and use cases defined.
- If the system does not perform as it should, the participant marks that response as a **Fail**, and (perhaps) writes a comment describing what went wrong.

The **development team** wants to make sure that the product works as expected.

- The team needs to know that when average people use the product, the product meets their requirements.
- **Before the test**, the team sets up the product for the particular test by creating sample data, preparing certain files, basically making up anything that the test participant will need to work with, during testing. (You describe these presets as "preconditions.")

- **During the test**, the team often watches the test participant very carefully, intervening if trouble strikes, asking questions, trying to understand what the test participant thought was going on, struggling to figure out what could possibly have gone wrong.

- **After a test** in which the product failed to do what it was supposed to, the team huddles, and works to fix the bug. Then they run the test again, to make sure that the bug is really squashed.

For both audiences, you need to include a lot more detail than you could back when you were writing a use case.

- You're helping the test participant know exactly what to do.

- You're helping the developers figure out what the test participant did, just before the bug struck. And you are discovering exactly when and what failed. In that way, the testing makes it easier to reproduce the bug, the first step in figuring out how to get rid of it.

- You have a real interface now, with menus, links, buttons, icons, tabs, and so on, and you want to make sure that it is all working correctly.

- You have real functionality underneath the hood—calculations, database queries, validations of data entry such as dates, phone numbers, saves.

- You know what **should** happen in areas that the user can see (the interface) and in areas that go on inside the computer (the functions). Your test case, if successful, confirms that in fact the system is working as planned, and it is delivering the correct results.

Sample test case

The following example of a test case is based on the sample use case in our previous module. But unlike our approach in the use case, we make the actions and results much more specific, for testing purposes, and we describe the actual interface.

TC15: Start a claim for loss
Related requirements:

> CR 1.   For each new claim, the system must assign a number.
>
> CR 2.   A policy must define the types of claims that may be made against the policy.
>
> CR 3.   Each claim must have a type.
>
> CR 4.   The system must verify that a claimant has a policy that covers the type of claim being made.
>
> CR 5.   The system must offer a list of adjusters within a 50-mile radius of the location of the claim.
>
> CR 6.   The system must offer the clerk the opportunity to review the draft claim before finalizing it.
>
> CR 7.   The system must notify the agent of a new claim against a policy issued by the agent.
>
> CR 8.   The system must notify the adjuster assigned to a claim.
>
> CR 9.   When finalized, the claim must be stored in the claims database.

Actors

- The claims clerk
- The insurance agent
- The claims adjuster
- The customer who is making the claim

Preconditions

The clerk is logged into the Claim Capture program.

The network is live.

The program has access to the databases of agents, adjusters, and claims, and they are functioning.

Write a Use Case

The system is at the home page, which includes a New Claim button.

A dummy policy has been set up, with the number P4335, which covers claims of loss. The insured is named Allison Gibbons, at 23 Bethune Street, New York, New York, 10001. The type of policy is Personal Property. It covers loss due to fire, storm, or theft.

There are phone numbers in the system for the agent, adjuster, and customer on policy P4335, so the system can text them at the end of the test case. Our test team has the phones with those numbers in hand.

Scenario:

The clerk creates a new claim in the system

Steps

Step	Actor	User action	Expected Result	Pass/Fail
TC15-1	Clerk	On the home page of the application, click New Claim.	You see an alert box, with a field labeled Policy Number, and the message, "Please enter the policy number for this claim." There is a Submit button underneath the field.	☐ Pass ☐ Fail
TC15-2	Clerk	Enter the policy number, P4335 and click Submit.	You see the following information about Policy P4335: • The insured is named Allison Gibbons, at 23 Bethune Street, New York, New York, 10001. • The type of policy is Personal Property. • It covers loss due to fire,	☐ Pass ☐ Fail

6. Creating a test case

			storm, or theft. You also see the question: "Which type of claim is this?" There are three buttons: Fire, Storm, Theft.	
TC15-3	Clerk	Click Theft.	You see a claim form, with a Submit button at the bottom. These fields are prefilled: • Policy Number: P4335 • Insured Person: Allison Gibbons • Home Address: 23 Bethune Street, New York, New York, 10001. • Policy Type: Personal Property. • Coverage: loss due to fire, storm, or theft. • Agent: George Brokers, Inc. There are also blank fields for • Date of incident • Location street • Location city • Location ZIP	☐ Pass ☐ Fail

139

			• Description of incident • Claimant • Customer estimate of value at loss	
TC15-4	Clerk	Fill in these fields: • Date of incident: June 23, 2016 • Location street: 23 Bethune Street • Location city: New York City • Location ZIP: 100001 • Description of incident. Man with a knife held her up in the front hall of her apartment building, took her wallet, fled on foot. Police report NYPD 55-A-14. • Claimant: Allison Gibbons	You see a claim number appear, with a list of adjusters near the location of the incident, asking the clerk to choose one: • Max Feldstein, 11 Washington Square Park • Herman Davis, 13 Little West 12th Street • Beverly Ward, 450 West 23rd Street	☐ Pass ☐ Fail

6. Creating a test case

		• Customer estimate of loss: $250. Then click Submit.		
TC15-5	Clerk	Choose Max Feldstein as the adjuster.	You see a message saying, "Max Feldstein is currently available; do you want to confirm this assignment?" Two buttons say: Confirm and Cancel.	☐ Pass ☐ Fail
TC15-6	Clerk	Click Confirm.	You see the message: "Do you want to review this claim before submitting it?" Two buttons say Yes or No.	☐ Pass ☐ Fail
TC15-7	Clerk	Click Yes.	You see all the information that you have just entered, and a Submit button.	☐ Pass ☐ Fail
TC15-8	Clerk	Confirm that the information is exactly as you entered it, then click Submit.	You see a message saying, "This claim has been submitted. Notices are being sent to the agent, the customer, and the adjuster." Underneath the message is the welcome screen.	☐ Pass ☐ Fail
	Agent		You see a text message saying, "A claim is being made against a policy that you issued, #P4335. Please check the Claims Database for details."	☐ Pass ☐ Fail
	Adjuster		You see a text message saying, "You have been assigned as an adjuster	☐ Pass ☐ Fail

			for a claim being made against a policy #P4335. Please check the Claims Database for details."	
	Customer		You see a message saying "We have received your claim of loss under policy P4335. Our adjuster, Max Feldstein, will be contacting you soon to learn more about the loss."	☐ Pass ☐ Fail

Test results

Here are some examples of the bugs that showed up during the testing.

- In Step 1, the word *policy* was misspelled in the label and the message.
- In Step 2, the system brought up the right customer, but the wrong policy type, saying this is a Workman's Comp policy.
- In step 3, the following fields were not prefilled: Home Address and Agent.
- In step 4, no claim number appeared.
- In step 4, the system provided adjustors from Arizona, not New York.
- In step 6, there was only one button, and it said Yes.
- In step 8, the adjuster did not receive any message.
- In step 8, the customer received the same message that was sent to the agent.

You can see how important it is to include the full details, so that the test participant can check whether or not the software is doing exactly what it should. Without specifics, the test would never have revealed these bugs.

Why do we test?

To prove that the product meets requirements

Practically speaking, we test to **find defects**, so we can fix them before we release the product.

We also test to **validate** that the product meets the real needs of the customers, not just the specs. Toward this end, we bring in real users to test usability and functionality—from the user's point of view.

In this way, testing helps us **reduce** the number of calls to support, and **increase** customer satisfaction, leading, we hope, to more sales.

To ensure quality

We test the product in many different ways, to identify problems. Then we fix those. Then we test again.

In the end, we want to achieve that mysterious state known as **quality**.

But how can we do that?

What is quality?

Definition in Rational Unified Process:

> "A product that is produced by an agreed-upon, repeatable, and managed process, and...
>
> "A product that meets or exceeds agreed-upon requirements, as measured by agreed-upon measures and criteria."

Your whole team has to focus on the goal: delivering quality products that meet the customer's real needs— on time and on budget.

> As a writer, you are one of the main advocates for the customer. So you have to do what you can to keep improving quality. One of those efforts is to develop good **test cases**.

The definition of quality has evolved. In the past, quality was defined as

- Satisfying the requirements documents.

    Even if they no longer apply; even if they do not really reflect what users need now.

- Passing a system test.

    Matching the code to the requirement documents, not necessarily making it reflect what users need.

- Making sure that development followed a process.

  But that assumes the process guarantees that you will meet stakeholder needs.

Now, quality means achieving the results that the users need (Return on Investment).

- Understanding what the stakeholders require from a system to solve a problem, satisfy a desire, or take advantage of an opportunity.

- Continually reviewing and getting feedback to refine the requirements, during each iteration.

- Confirming that the stakeholders are getting full value for their money, and full functionality as planned.

Quality shows up in several dimensions.

Here are some aspects of quality.

1. Reliability
2. Performance
3. Supportability
4. *Functionality*
5. *Usability*

As test writers, we care most about the two dimensions known as *functionality* and *usability*, but many of the other aspects of quality raise their heads, if users encounter problems during the tests.

Testing tells you whether your product is doing what you said it would.

- The product is **reliable**. It does not crash.

- It holds up under heavy use. Its **performance** is acceptable.

- It works in installations and configurations you planned for. You can **support** it.

- It lets users do what they hoped to do. It **functions**.

- It is easy for the target audience to use. It's **usable**.

But testing is hard.

- You cannot find **all** the problems that a user may encounter.

- You do not know where the bugs are until you test.

- You cannot predict how long it will take to fix one set of problems, and then test the fixes.

So testing is **iterative**.

- You find a bug, you fix it, you test…and discover that in fixing that problem, you broke something else. So you have to fix that and test again.
- Just repairing one problem may take three or four rounds of testing.
- You have to prioritize the problems: Which ones are most important to your users? You may have to postpone fixing some because you do not have time or money to debug them.
- It's common for a major piece of software to ship with several thousand "known bugs."

Testing often eats up 30% to 50% of the development budget. But when only the developers test their own code, they miss a lot. So as a team, you must:

- Develop a formal method for testing with real users—and without.
- Use automation to improve productivity and efficiency in tests that do not require real users.
- To test usability and functionality on real users, create scenarios and tasks that lead them to take actions you can observe.
- Track the quantity and seriousness of all defects discovered during testing.
- Fix the worst problems, and test again…and again…and again.

As a writer, you will probably be most involved with two kinds of testing: Functional Testing and Usability Testing. But you need to recognize that these are only part of the testing that must go on, to assure quality.

Five ways we test for quality

As a writer, you hear a lot about testing, but you contribute the most to the testing that involves real users, whether in person or at a distance (remotely). To be clear, we need to distinguish what we do from other forms of testing, most of which are done by the development team and quality assurance folks, out of our sight.

1. Reliability tests

Goal: Verify that the application does not fail during execution, leading to crashes, hangs, memory leaks, or data corruption.

These tests are run by developers impromptu during development, then formally when an iteration nears the end of development.

We're asking questions such as:

- How often does it fail?
- What's the mean time between failures?
- How bad are the crashes?
- How well does the software recover after a failure?
- Are the results of calculations accurate?
- Do the database lookups return the right data?
- What kind of volume can the software handle?

Generally these tests are automated. But when we bring users in to try out the software, we sometimes encounter crashes, or other symptoms of unreliability.

2. Performance tests

Goal: Under a production load, verify that the system performs its functions, and does not fail.

These tests are run by the developers or quality assurance folks near the end of development, asking questions such as:

- Does it perform within acceptable limits, under normal volumes, edge conditions?
- Does it meet benchmarks?
- Is the software relatively efficient?
- How fast is it to respond to user input?
- Is it becoming a resource hog?
- How's the throughput?

Generally these tests are automated, without user input.

3. Supportability tests

Goal: Verify that the application can actually be supported, later, when installed.

Usually these tests are run by developers or quality assurance teams, to make sure that the software installs properly, without knocking anything down, or hanging up. Users are rarely involved, though they probably should be.

Some questions we are exploring:

- Does the software install compatibly on each kind of system it will be used on?
- Do the configuration options work correctly?
- Can the software be distributed and installed remotely?
- Is it relatively easy to localize?
- Is the software designed to be easy to maintain?

4. Functional tests

Goal: Verify that the system functions as intended.

We want to exercise every use case, and touch every feature, to make sure that the system is doing what we planned for. Questions we are exploring:

- Does it work as intended?
- Where do ordinary users get tangled up?
- Do calculations come up with the right results?

We write test cases so that users can run through the scenarios, to see if the system responds as expected. In each scenario, the user must perform one or more tasks while we and other folks watch.

Many of these tests are done **in person** with users, with developers and you hovering nearby, to make sure everything is ready. Any defects discovered go immediately to developers to fix, or to the project team to analyze and schedule for another iteration.

Other forms of functional testing are done using software to track user behavior. (You may prepare a description of what you hope users will do, and how we can tell, but you do not personally observe users at work in front of you.)

In-Person Observation

You prepare a series of steps in which the test participant must do an action, followed by a description of what the system should do in response.

You watch as people go through the steps. They mark each step as a Pass or Fail, depending on whether the system has done what you thought it would, or not.

Later, you may also talk with participants about their experiences, to see what was confusing.

Talk-Aloud

You ask the user to talk while working on the task.

The payoff: You hear what they are thinking, what they are puzzled by, what frustrates them…at the same time that you see what they are doing.

Some people can do this easily; others cannot. But when the user can talk freely, you learn a lot about problems with the interface, the functionality, the instructions you wrote.

In situations where you need to write a report pointing to problems, and offering suggested solutions, you may need to create a complete transcript of everything that you and the test participants said, then do "**protocol analysis**" on that (extensive) text. Of course, that takes a lot more time. So most teams settle for listening to what people say on the fly, making quick notes, and then discussing those at a team meeting the next day.

Eye Tracking

You track the eye movements of the users doing tasks that you have laid out. You can see where their attention is going, moment by moment.

This approach is particularly useful when testing navigation, graphic layouts, and content on a web site.

You learn even more if you are in the room, to watch what they do, and then talk with them about what they experienced.

Remote Testing

In companies where the users are in one country, and the development team is in another, you can watch users remotely, via video conferencing or screen-sharing software, as they perform tasks that you describe for them.

Unfortunately, you cannot see their body language very well, if at all; and you may not be able to get very helpful information from post-test interviews.

(Users may be a bit intimidated, and their replies can often be formal, and correct, hiding any problems that they encountered).

A/B Testing

In developing or revising a web site, we often do A/B testing, where we put up one version on the site for a period, then another; or we show one version to one group of users, and the other version to another group.

Because we can get rapid feedback from a lot of people, we can tell which approach leads to a result we want, such as increased sales, fewer abandoned shopping carts, more people completing the purchase funnel, more time on site.

This kind of testing goes on online, so you only get to see statistical results. You may have no idea why one version works better, but the statistics prove it does.

Clickstream Analysis

This approach tells us the sequence of options, screens, or pages that users visit, click by click, as they use a site or software product.

We are not present; we are using software to make the record, and we have to work hard to make sense of the statistics. But we usually have no direct contact with the users.

Scripts

Developers often set up scripts that test key aspects of the functionality, long before you do user testing. These scripts run a series of challenges to the system, putting in good and bad data to see how it reacts.

Does the system correctly look up a login, for example, or refuse to accept a word as a date?

For example:

```
*** Test Case ***
Valid Login
    [Documentation]     Opens a browser to login url, inputs username
    ...                 and password and checks the welcome page is
open.
    ...                 This is a smoke test. Created in iteration 3.
    Open Browser        ${URL}   ${BROWSER}
    Input Text          field1   ${UN11}
    Input Text          field2   ${PW11}
    Click Button        button_12
    Title Should Be     Welcome Page
    [Teardown]          Close Browser
```

Early testing smokes out serious errors, failures to validate, incorrect calculations; thus, smoke tests check whether a module is so badly broken that it would make no sense to do any user testing.

To make sure that the software is catching all the possible errors that a user might make when entering information, scripts send bad data, such as

- For a number field: words, letters, nothing entered, all zeroes, negative numbers
- For a text field: nothing but white space, illegal values, special characters, foreign characters
- For value lists: nothing selected, combination selected, all items selected
- For file uploads: an empty file (0 bytes), a huge file, a very long file name, an illegal file name

As a writer, you do not have to create these scripts. Hopefully, by the time that you bring in some users to do testing under your eye, the worst errors and malfunctions have been fixed.

5. Usability tests

Goal: Evaluate the experience of using the system, from the user's point of view.

We set up challenges, and without providing specific instructions, we ask users to do those tasks, to see if they can navigate the software on their own.

As in functional testing, we prepare a set of scenarios, describing realistic situations, and setting out a series of tasks for the user to accomplish with our product. But we do not offer step-by-step instructions. Can people find their own way, without us?

We see users encounter problems with the look and feel of the user interface, the consistency of the buttons, menus, and forms, the degree to which the functionality maps to the conceptual models that users bring to bear. We are observing and sometimes talking with real users as they experience the software.

Usability testing sometimes reaches beyond the application itself to include:

- Online and context-sensitive help
- Wizards and agents
- User documentation
- Training materials

Because these tests aim at finding out how well real people can use the software, teams often prefer to test in person, rather than automate the testing.

But in some circumstances, we start by bringing in **experts** in user interface and usability to review the software, identifying potential problems based on experience and guidelines. They usually start with a set of guidelines or criteria, known as *heuristics*, and note deviations. This approach, known as a **heuristic evaluation**, checks standards such as those that Jakob Nielsen advocated in these areas:

- Visibility of System Status
- Match Between System and the Real World
- User Control and Freedom
- Consistency and Standards
- Error Prevention
- Recognition Rather Than Recall
- Flexibility and Efficiency of Use
- Aesthetic and Minimalist Design
- Help Users Recognize, Diagnose, and Recover from Errors
- Help and Documentation

You may have sessions just devoted to usability issues, or you may just be watching for these problems during the functional testing.

What's NOT testing?

- Talking to people about a future product.
- Convening a focus group to explore attitudes toward your product, or your competitors.
- Exploring the why and how of decision making.
- Audience definition. (This analysis should have happened long ago).

Testing saves money.

- A software problem can be 100 to 1000 times as expensive to find and fix after you have deployed the software.
- Therefore your team needs to test every iteration, using as much automation as possible, to increase productivity and effectiveness.
- In each iteration, you should also be testing against the cumulative set of requirements.

Why have the users test the functionality and usability?

- To catch and fix mistakes before release.
- To identify and repair confusing aspects of the navigation or interface before release.
- To correct errors, gaps, or inconsistency in any data that gets displayed to the users.

Only users can prove that your application functions for them as designed.

User testing of functionality and usability is different from other kinds of testing. You are submitting the product or site to real people, to see if they find it understandable, usable…even useful.

Finding users to test the software

Recruit real users—or people very much like them so that you can be sure the software will work for them. It's cheating to bring in an assortment of programmers and tech writers, claiming, "Well, we know what they want."

Create a user profile and make sure everyone matches it.

- Level of knowledge of the domain
- Level of experience with this software, or competing products
- Level of experience in one of the roles you want them to play
- Ability to show up on time, and attend for the full session

To persuade people to participate:

- Promise them chocolate (excellent technique)

- Indicate that this is one way that they can influence the evolving software (pretty persuasive, in some circumstances)
- Get their managers to require attendance (Weak, results in surly attendees)
- Rent them from a temp agency (But only if you can afford it, and you can get the agency to guarantee that the people match your profile)
- Pay them directly (great if you have the budget, and there is no other way to bring the folks in off the street)

How many users?

In general, it's better to have a small group do a test, then fix the product, then have another small group do the next test.

Four or five people—that's enough to expose 80% of the problems in one session.

Jakob Nielsen jokingly called this "Quick and Dirty" testing. He made a good statistical argument for this approach, saying:

> "Elaborate usability tests are a waste of resources. The best results come from testing no more than five users and running as many small tests as you can afford."

Scheduling the user test sessions

The schedule depends on the process you develop.

Are you going to test one person at a time, or several people at once?

If you care most about proving that the software functions as required, you can have a mass testing. You are mostly asking: does the system do what it is supposed to?

If you also care about the user experience, consider testing one person at a time. In this environment, you can observe the person's reactions very closely, and understand why confusion arises. You can also do substantial debriefing, asking what they felt, where they got confused—key information for identifying defects in usability.

Doing the tests one at a time yields much more valuable information on usability, but eats up a lot of time--for you and for the developer who has to set up and monitor the condition of the system.

Who should be watching?

Ideally, **you** should observe. You learn

- What you left out of your instructions
- Where your writing is ambiguous
- What problems people have with the interface
- What people think is going on (their conceptual model)
- What their real-life situations are (the context in which they may use the software)

A **developer** must be available:

- To prepare the data to be used in the tests.
- To direct people to the right version of the software (often in a directory that most users never see, with a name like Quality).
- To troubleshoot problems with logging in, setting up user roles, stumbling over the interface.
- To walk a user through a problem, to understand what the root cause is, right at that moment, when the user is available, and the system is in the exact state that led to the blowup.

A **project manager** or **marketing maven** would be good, too. You want to give them the chance to see real users struggling to do tasks that are like their real work.

When should you test?

Ideally, the iteration has a few days at the end for quality assurance (particularly the automated tests for performance, reliability, and supportability) and your kind of testing (functionality and usability). You need to leave enough time after testing for the developers to fix the problems.

If the bug fixes are complex, you'll need to test again before release.

Do you have a space?

Who is reserving the room?

What computers are there?

In that space, on those computers, can these users actually tap into your network, or do you need to launch the application from a phone?

Do you have developers?

Who is going to be preparing the systems, so that all the preconditions are met?

It's very good for developers to watch people suffer with their code.

Preparing to test usability

To test usability, keep it simple.

Start with a goal that your users might really get behind.

Pose a real goal, but one that is open to personal interpretation. Examples:

- Buy a scarf for under $100.
- Pick a movie that you would like to see next Sunday afternoon.
- Create a job posting for someone who will be your assistant.

Leave the small stuff to the user. The more you give them freedom to choose, the more motivated they are.

Make the goal something that they might really want to do, and that they might really do. If you make up an outlandish goal, or one that is clearly silly, they will not be able to "believe" in what they are doing, and your results will be skewed toward fantasy.

Urge them to act.

Do not ask them to talk about what they **would** do. Have them do it.

> "The most effective way of understanding what works and what doesn't in an interface is to watch people use it. ...

> "If you ask, 'How would you find a way to do X?' or 'Tell me how you would do Y' the participant is likely to answer in words, not actions. And unfortunately, people's self-reported data is not as accurate as when they actually use a system."

> —"Turn User Goals into Task Scenarios for Usability Testing," NN Group

In a usability test, do not tell them what to click.

You want to see what they will pick, how they will navigate. Do not tip your hand. For this kind of test, you cannot specify what elements of the user interface to use.

For example, if you tell the user to click the Tools menu, you won't find out whether the user could locate the particular item that you want to test.

By contrast: In a functionality test, we tell them in great detail exactly what parts of the interface to use, and what exactly to expect as a result.

Unlike functional testing, usability testing does not describe every step.

It sets goals, and suggests tasks, but it does not make sure that every step in the use case is functioning correctly. We leave that kind of testing to the more formal test cases of functionality, which are based directly on your use cases.

Preparing to test functionality

Be complete. You are going to provide more detail than you would in a usability test, more detail than you would put into a task topic or procedure.

Create a test case for each scenario that will be implemented in the iteration.

Here, for example, is a list of scenarios for an iteration. We would create a test case for each one.

```
Use Case: Start a Work Plan
```
- ```
  Start a work plan: Basic Flow
  ```
- ```
  Unknown organization: Basic Flow,
  Unknown Organization
  ```
- ```
  Status incomplete: Basic Flow, Work
  Plan Status Check
  ```
- ```
  Permit list incomplete: Basic Flow,
  Questions, Status Check
  ```

```
Use Case: Identify Hazards
```
- ```
  Open a Hazard Analysis: Basic Flow
  ```
- ```
  Hazard analysis incomplete: Basic
  Flow, Hazard Analysis Status Check
  ```
- ```
  Training records not available: Basic
  Flow, Training System Unavailable
  ```
- ```
  Technical Work Documents not
  available: Basic Flow, TWD System
  unavailable
  ```

You may be testing an entire use case (all scenarios), or just select scenarios from a use case.

In many situations, one iteration handles the entire use case, including the basic flow, any subflows, and all the alternative flows, just because that is a coherent bundle of functionality for the developers to produce.

But if a use case is particularly gnarly, the team may decide to do the basic flow in one iteration, and others later.

You are developing a way to test what the team has developed, from a user's point of view. And you are testing the way the system responds to the user in the situations described by the scenarios.

Your project team sets the schedule for developing the test cases.

- On some teams, the use cases give the developers enough information to start coding. In this situation, you create the test cases as they code, so you will be ready to test in the last week or two of the iteration.

- Other times, developers look to the test cases as specs—what they must code to. So you have to develop the test cases as soon as the team has identified the functions to be developed in the next iteration—probably a few weeks before the developers start to code.

Typical components of a functional test case

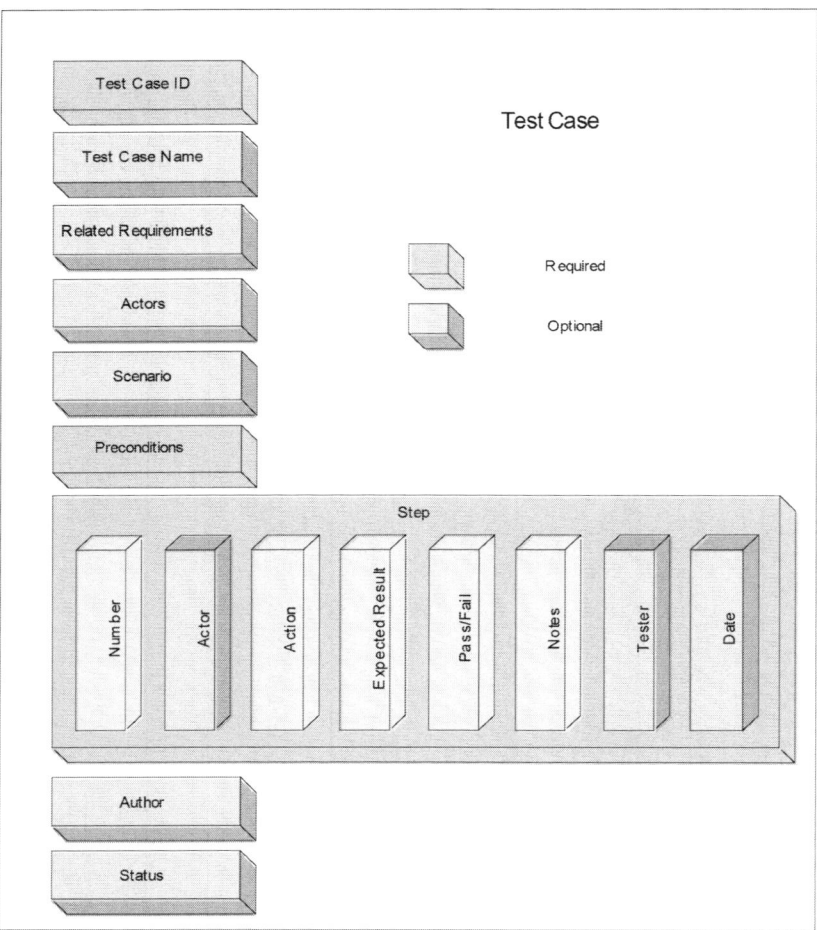

Write a complete test case for each scenario.

In functional testing, we test every step in the use case, to make sure that in fact the system functions as designed. (This goal is very different from the more open-ended usability testing we just looked at).
IEEE standard 829-1998 defines a test case as an input and an expected result. But we usually expand on that pattern. Here are the elements you need to consider for your test cases.

Test Case ID

The ID is useful when your team has to talk quickly about a bunch of test cases. It is convenient to make the ID of the test case echo the ID for the use case it comes from.

Example: If your scenario is UC45S2a, then you may want to make your Test Case ID something like UC45TC2a. You need to tie the test case directly to a specific scenario, within a particular use case, and the ID is one way to do that.

Test Case Name

Echo the name of the scenario as closely as you can.

> If the name of the scenario is Reject Ownership, make the name of the test case Reject Ownership.

Err on the side of completeness. The name helps test participants understand the goal of the actions they will take, and helps developers trace the test case back to a particular scenario within a use case

Related Requirements

Depending on how far back your team needs to trace the functionality, you could add a section like this, to include material from earlier artifacts:

- User needs (rare, because these are so vague)

- Features (more common, because these are general statements of what the system will do, without some of the precision and jargon of actual requirement statements)

- Functional requirements statements with their original ID numbers (frequent)

- Business rules (common, but hard to distinguish from regular requirements statements).

You generally do **not** include design constraints here. (Those are descriptions of the way the software must be developed, and specs for the user interface).

You do **not** include non-functional requirements (aka "supplementary requirements") in the test case, because the team should be testing for those on their own, without bothering the test participants.

Caution: Do not modify the language of the functional requirement statement. You must quote it exactly.

Actors

Often there is only one actor, that is, the person who starts the ball rolling. Remember that the name of the actor is all you need. It is a role, not a person; and no more than a role.

Just the names of the roles. No need for detailed descriptions here.

Do not describe the actual test participants. You may talk about them in your test plan, but not here. Here the **actor** is the role that you planned for, back when you were writing the use case.

In a test case, we do not bother mentioning other systems as actors. We are concerned here with the roles of the humans who will be exercising the test case.

But sometimes there are two or more different people who are involved in some kind of complex exchange of information. In that situation, we need to list these roles, and give them their chance to act in the test case.

If your whole suite of test cases relies on a single actor (one role) throughout, then you can probably skip the Actor column. But if different scenarios are exercised by different human actors, or if one scenario involves two or more people, you probably do need to identify who acts in which step. Then you need an Actors column. (For your own sanity, later, when you are combing over the marked-up test cases to see what went wrong, knowing who did what is very helpful.)

> ### Missing actor:
>
> ```
> Step 3: The aircraft system result: The system
> now informs the ground administrator that an
> alert is about to be transmitted from the
> plane.
>
> Step 4: The ground administrator confirms
> receipt of the alert.
> ```
>
> > What's wrong?
> >
> > So far, your only actor has been the pilot of the plane. But the pilot cannot confirm that the ground administrator has received this alert.
> >
> > You want to know whether or not that alert came through.
> >
> > Better: Create a second actor, the Ground Administrator. Have a real person act in this role, so that she can confirm that, yes, a message came through from the plane.
> >
> > Moral: Whenever your system involves an exchange between

two people, they should probably both be actors. That is why we may need the column for actors.

Relevant Scenario

To tie this test case to a specific use case and scenario, you may want to add this component. Just name the scenario.

- Do not summarize all the steps of the test case. You are not being asked to give a plot summary of the test case.
- Just name the scenario you are referring to back in the use case.
- One scenario per test case.

Remember: Each scenario gets its own separate test case.

Preconditions or Setup

The preconditions include all the ones described in the use case. But there are probably going to be others, because you are setting up the test devices and any files that the test participants may need.

Example:

You need to prepare the system to recognize a user named ABC, with a password of XYZ. And later your steps need to tell that user to enter the username ABC and a password of XYZ.

If you are not specific in the setup, as described in Preconditions, and in steps, the developer may not really be able to debug any failures with the login function.

So your preconditions would say: "There is an established user with the user name of ABC, whose password is XYZ."

You may need to put the system into a particular mode, or prepare other conditions for the test.

This section is really for the developers, reminding them of what they have to do ahead of time, to make the test work.

Bad example of a precondition:

```
The user is aware of the video options.
```

What's wrong with this?

Preconditions should describe the setup of the system, not the level of awareness in the user.

Better:

Drop this precondition altogether.

Bad example of a precondition:

```
There is a file with a square in it.
```

What's wrong with this?

> What is the file name? Where is it? How can the user find it? What kind of an object is inside?

We need all this information for testing. We want to make sure that when the user opens the file, the user sees what we put into it, exactly. No errors.

So we need to give very detailed descriptions of what we are setting up.

Better:

```
In the Objects folder, there is a file called
SquareOne, which contains a single object, a
square measuring 2 inches on each side, with
the line stroke of 1.25 points, and no fill.
```

Bad example of a precondition:

```
There is a record describing the employee's
home address.
```

What's wrong with this?

The team needs to set up the record before the test. So you have to say what should go into each field.

That way, later, the test participant can tell you whether that specific record is discoverable in the database, and whether all that information is coming through correctly or not. These are the kind of functions that we want to test.

Better:

```
There is a record for the employee Julian
Johnson.  It includes this information: Full
Name: Julian Johnson; Honorific: Dr.; Street
Address: 67 Bethune Lane; Apartment: #43;
City: New York City; State: New York; ZIP:
10001.
```

Good examples of preconditions or setup:

- The User Login of Admin, password Host, is associated with the role of Super User.
- The system is already in Report Mode at the start of the test.
- The user Herb Simon has been assigned a corrective action plan that specifies that an external verifier will be required.
- The Admin's username is Algernon_Swinburne, and the password is Elegance1837!.
- The network is functioning, and the AR database is active.

Steps

Here you tell the user what to do, describe the expected result (the system response), and ask the user to record whether the system passed or failed.

This part of the test case is essentially a form on which the user can record success or failure.

Each component of a step appears in its own **column**, from left to right across the page.

- Number (Required)
- Actor (Optional)
- Action (Required)
- Expected Results (Required)
- Pass/Fail (Required)
- Notes or Comments (Optional)
- Tester Name (Optional)
- Test Date (Optional)

Number

As in a regular procedure, you number the steps to show the order in which they should be performed.

Here, though, your numbers may be composite. For instance, if your scenario is S6, and your test case is TC6, your steps might be TC6-1, TC6-2, and so on.

Actor

You include this column only if you have several actors in the test case, such as an Administrator and an Employee.

Example:

> Most of the actions in a test case are performed by the Clerk. But those actions are triggered by a request from a Traveler, and at the end of the test case, a specific message goes back to the Traveler.
>
> To make this work in a test situation, you need to have the Traveler send the request, and then you need to have the Traveler read the message, and confirm that it says what the Clerk wrote. So in two of your rows, you would have the Traveler as actor. To show that, you would use the Actor column.

Action

What the test participant who is acting as the **actor** for this step **should** do.

How many actions per step?

What governs the number of user actions in a single step is the expected result. You have to have people do whatever it takes to generate some response from the system. If that takes three steps, you write the three steps in a single cell, as a, b, and c, because only after c does the system come alive, and give an expected result.

> **Note**: This approach is different from a regular procedure, where you would give a separate numbered step to each meaningful action the user should take.

Write the actions in the imperative, just as you would in a procedure.

> When developers write test cases, you often see the actions described in third-person narratives. ("The user selects…the user enters…the user saves.") But in the test session, you want the participant to carry out these actions, so using the imperative is clearer. Do this, and do that.

Describe the user interface exactly, because **now** you have an interface to describe. (When you wrote the use case, there was no user interface, so you were purposefully vague, to allow the developers to come up with the best design).

- If someone has to pick a date from a calendar picker, say *pick*, or *select*.
- If someone types text into a text box, that is *typing* or *entering*...not *selecting*.
- If they choose something from a menu, that is *choosing*, not *selecting*.
- When the user picks a word or image to work on, that is *selecting*.

Make sure that each step is really testable.

- Can we really tell if it passed or failed?
- Are your instructions specific enough, so the user could not just improvise? (If the user has a lot of freedom, then the developers may never know what the user did, that brought down the system.)
- Err on the side of completeness, detail, and precision. Be bossy. Tell the user exactly what to do, so that the developers know just what the user was doing that led to an error, or crash.
- Without specificity, you are not really testing the system in a way that gives useful results to the developers.

Don't leave out any actions that the user must perform to get to the "result" that you expect.

- If you don't have much experience in writing procedures, slow down. Try describing just what happens, moment to moment, in an Apple or Microsoft application, then compare that with the Help, to see what another professional has done. Notice that in general, if the user must do something, the procedure says so.
- If you leave an action up to the whim of the user, you have lost control. Your developers won't be able to debug when a problem arises, because you won't have given the user explicit directions, and you have left out a key user action. Who knows if the user really did it?

Good actions:

- Select the file named InventoryControl and click Open.
- Type the message: Signal outage discovered next to Rio Rancho station. Please send a repair crew to 2131 La Mancha Road.
- Open the Photos folder.
- In the third line, choose the Gift Wrapping option.

Bad action:

Choose a tool.

What's wrong with this?

It is not specific. The user can pick any tool. In that situation, the developers do not know which tool the user picked, and therefore they cannot figure out what the user did, if it led to disaster.

Better:

Choose the Rectangle tool.

Bad action:

Look at the screen.

What's wrong with that?

The action does not trigger any response from the system. We are interested in actions that should, if all is going well, provoke a function.

This kind of placeholder action often comes up when we have the user do something that provokes multiple system responses, and we want the user to check each one. The solution: Instead of creating a bogus user action (looking), list all of those responses in the cell for Expected Results in the row where the user actually acts on the system.

Occasionally, we reach for the "Look and see" action when we have results that affect two different actors. Solution: Within the same step, create a new row for the second actor, and give that person nothing to do, but display the result that this person would see. The second test participant can then confirm that the system is displaying exactly what we think it should show that actor.

Bad action:

>   Use the microphone to dictate a note.

What's wrong with that?

We do not tell the test participant what to say. So we do not know what should appear in the note. And therefore we cannot test whether the voice recognition is working correctly. And when we send the note to someone else, and have that other person check it, we have no way of telling whether it came through correctly.

In other words, we cannot test the result.

Better:

>   Use the microphone to dictate a note
>   that says, "The water level at sluice
>   gate 34 is four feet below flood
>   level."

Expected Result

What we expect that the system will do in response to the action.

Note that in a regular procedure, you might leave out a result statement if it is obvious or routine, but in the test case you must include every result that a user should witness. The whole point of the test is to see if the system responds as it is supposed to.

Write these as you would in a procedure. For example, you would say, "The Solution Detail window appears," not "The system displays the Solution Detail window."

Generally there is only one response from the system. But if you have several responses all at once (cancelling the account, sending out an email to the customer, notifying the credit manager), include them all in the one cell. (You can't create a new row, because the extra responses do not stem from any additional action on the user's part, and you are not asking a second actor to do anything).

Bad result:

>   You see a list of options.

Which options? How can the test participant tell if the right options came up? How can the developers tell if the right set of options really did come up?

Better:

> You see a list that shows three
> items: SmartArt, SmartChart, and
> SmartTable.

Bad result:

> You see the personnel record.

What's wrong with this?

We are testing to make sure that the system displays the right information in the right order in this record. So we need to tell the participant what we think should appear.

Better:

> You see a personnel record titled
> Linda H. Greenhouse, with only two
> fields filled in. The Employee ID is
> 3545. The security level is Top
> Secret. The fields that are empty
> are: SSIN_Last4, Department, Hire
> Date, Current Status, and Benefits
> Package. At the top of the record, on
> the right, you see links to Personally
> Identifiable Information, Training
> Records, Management Reviews, Safety
> Records, and Payroll Records.

Bad result:

> You see the G logo in green.

What's wrong with this?

In the next step, you expect the user to click the OFF icon, which appears on top of the green logo. But you never mentioned that OFF icon in this result.

So the developers will not be sure that it came up as planned. Remember that we need to say exactly what we think should happen, so that the participant can confirm that. Without details, the participant cannot give us the information we need, and we may miss a crucial bug.

Better:

> You see the G logo in green, with an
> OFF icon on top of it, in a red box.

Bad result:

> You can now select a quantity.

What's wrong with this?

It does not describe the system's response to the user's last action. Instead, it talks about the user. And it **implies** that the system offers some kind of dialog or dropdown list with quantities. But we cannot be sure.

There is nothing to test, because the result statement fails to describe something that the user can see. Therefore the user cannot really decide whether the system has passed or failed.

Better:

> The system displays the number 1 in the Quantity box, with up and down arrows next to it.

Now the user can say, yes, there is the number, and yes, there are the arrows. OK, it passes.

And, in this way, the user can, in the next step, use the Up arrow to change the number in the Quantity box from 1 to 2.

Bad result:

> The device displays the message, "Please choose Black or Color."

What is wrong with this?

Well, in the next step, the user is going to tap a button called Black. But we did not ask the participant to confirm that in fact, in addition to the question, the system offered two buttons, one of which says *Black*, and other of which says *Color*.

So when we tell the user, "Tap Black," and the participant says that the action fails, we will not know whether the system just failed to act on the command, or if in fact there was no such button to tap.

From the point of view of a developer who is trying to figure out what went wrong, omitting the mention of the buttons means that the team lacks crucial information.

Better:

> The device displays the message, "Please choose Black or Color," and offers two buttons: Black, and Color.

Pass/Fail

Here you put two checkboxes, so the person doing the test can check off Pass or Fail.

If the system responds as expected, the person checks Pass. If not, Fail.

Later, when you are looking through all these forms for defects, a checkmark next to a Fail stands out.

Notes or Comments

You often learn a lot from what people enter here. You discover that your instruction was misleading, that the system displayed the wrong window, that the right message appeared but it included typos. You learn about quality problems and interface issues here. In the test room, you want to encourage people to make as many notes as they feel like.

Tester Name

Sometimes you need a column like this for the tester to initial, indicating who exactly ran this step, so you can ask them follow-up questions later.

Generally, though, the same person acts in the same role throughout the test case, and even throughout the test suite, so you just need a name on the top of the form.

Test Date

This column helps you identify which test session you are looking at. If you have three test sessions, defects get fixed after each one. So by the third session, you hope that problems revealed in the first test session have been resolved. The dates help you check on progress.

Bad Example of Steps

#	Actor	Action	Expected Result	Pass/Fail	Note	Name	Date
TC2 1-4	Engineer	Choose Location.	You see a list of buildings within the campus.	☐ Pass ☐ Fail			
TC2 1-5	Engineer	Select the building known as Beryllium Test Facility from the Location list.	You see a list of the workspaces and laboratories in that building.	☐ Pass ☐ Fail			

What's wrong with these steps?

In step TC2 1-4, the user action is clear, but the results are not. When four test participants marked this as Pass, then two others said it was a Fail, the engineers wanted to figure out what was going on. Turns out that the first four just saw a list, and figured, OK, that is a list, good enough. But the other two knew what buildings were on the campus, and noticed that the list contained a mix of building names and workspace names. These test participants said to themselves, "Wait, these are **not** all building names, so this result is a fail."

The last two participants were right. The system was randomly drawing names from two different tables. A serious error. But because the result cell did not list the actual buildings that ought to show up, the first four participants had no idea whether or not the list was right. If the test had ended with them, the development team would have thought that their queries to the database were working just fine.

In some situations, the system did display the Beryllium Test Facility in the list of buildings, but at other times it did not. So three of the test participants marked step 5 as Fail, because they could not choose that building, as specified in the user action. Three other test participants were able to choose that building. And each one got a list of workspaces and labs. One participant, who was new to the campus, gave the system a Pass, because, after all, some list came up. The other two participants gave the system a Fail on this step, because they knew that the workspaces that came up did not occur inside that building.

In this step, then, the developers might not have discovered that their queries were once again failing, except that two of the participants knew, from real life, what to expect. The test case would have been more reliable if the writer had included all the right workspaces in the statement of the expected result.

Revised steps

The team revised its queries, and the writer revised the Actions and Expected Results in the test case.

#	Actor	Action	Expected Result
TC21-4	Engineer	Choose Location.	You see this list of buildings within the campus: Headquarters, Air Lab, Crash Test Facility, Efficient Manufacturing, Beryllium Test Facility.
TC21-5	Engineer	Choose the building known as Beryllium Test Facility from the Location list.	You see a list of the workspaces and laboratories in that building: HazMat Station, Piping and Wiring Station, Robotic Chemistry Lab, Hazardous Physics Lab

This time, the test participants knew exactly what to look for, to confirm that the results were the ones expected. They were no longer guessing.

When the list of workspaces in the Beryllium Test Facility lacked the Robotic Chemistry Lab, all six participants spotted the error, and the development team could home in on the specific issue, and fix it.

For the next test, they were able to use the same test case again, and now both steps passed. Because the Results column was so specific, this last test gave the developers confidence that the participants were really getting the right results.

Good example of Actions and Results in Steps

#	Actor	Action	Expected Result
TC34-1	Proposed Owner	Click the link in the email notifying you that you are being proposed as the owner of a corrective action.	You see the Define Problem dialog, saying "You have been proposed as the owner of this corrective action," with the buttons for Accept or Reject ownership.
TC34-2	Proposed Owner	Click Reject.	You see a message confirming that you have rejected ownership. "You have rejected ownership of this corrective action. Do you want to Save?" There are two buttons: Save, and Cancel.
TC34-3	Proposed Owner	Click Save.	You return to the application home page, which says Welcome, with options for New CA, Existing CA, and Roles. The system confirms that it has saved your rejection. You receive an email titled Ownership Rejected; it says, "You have rejected ownership of this corrective action." A message titled Ownership Rejected goes to your immediate superior, Alvin Johnson.
TC34-4	Proposed Owner	Open your email application.	You see an email titled Ownership Rejected
TC34-5	Proposed Owner	Open the email titled Ownership Rejected.	It says: "You have rejected ownership of this corrective action (#55)."
TC34-6	Superior	Open your email program.	You see a message titled Ownership Rejected.
TC34-7	Superior	Open the email titled Ownership Rejected.	It says: "The proposed owner for the corrective action #55 has rejected ownership."

We write differently in a Test Case

Because a test is so different from a discussion of a future product, and because we are writing instructions for people to try out on the software, we must adapt our style, moving beyond the way we wrote the use case.

- We address the test participant directly, as you.
- We give instructions in the imperative.
- We describe the user interface in detail.

Each change in our style helps the developers spot the exact action that may have triggered an error, or, more happily, confirm when a specific action evokes the correct function, for all test participants. And in every step, we get a chance to confirm that all relevant elements of the user interface appear as planned.

Examples of moving style from a use case to a test case:

Element	Use Case	Test Case
Action	The user chooses to put a watermark on the image.	On the Insert menu, choose Watermark.
	The user chooses the option to create a table of contents.	On the Insert menu, choose Index and Tables. In the Index and Tables dialog, click the Table of Contents tab.
	The user chooses which style headings to include, indicating what level each one should have in the table of contents.	In the Table of Contents tab, click Options. In the Table of Contents Options dialog, make sure that Styles is checked. Next to the style Heading 1, enter a 1 in the text box. Next to the style Heading 2, enter a 2 in the text box. Click OK.
Results	The system displays the name of the caller, the phone number, a photo of the caller, and options to accept the call, text a reply, or send the call to voicemail.	You see that the caller is Bennett Cerf, calling from 212 233 4443, and his picture shows a man with red hair and a top hat. Underneath the picture you see the options Accept, Text Back, and Send to Voicemail.

6. Creating a test case

	The selected text takes on the color that the user picked.	The selected text turns red.
	The system shows the text to be found, the replacement text, and a list of all instances of the text to be found, with that text highlighted in context.	You see the word **Jerome** in the Find box at the top of the Find and Replace dialog, with an option to Find, and dropdown box with the icon of a gear. Below that, you see **Jerry** in the next box, with two buttons: Replace All, and Replace. Then in the area called Matches, you see the following: …tell **Jerome** to be careful with his inv.. …we need **Jerome** solvent if we are to… …please caution **Jerome** about this acc… The word Jerome is boldfaced and highlighted in yellow in each found passage.
	The system queries the transaction database using the customer account number as the key. The system displays the results of the query.	You see column headers: Trans. Date, Post Date, Description, Amount. Underneath those you see a boldfaced phrase: Standard Purchases Below that you see two transactions, separated by a horizontal line: 08/18 08/19 MICROSOFT Bellevue WA $98 08/18 08/19 ADOBE San Jose CA $275

Write a Use Case

Imagining your audiences

Remember that you are always writing with two different groups in mind.

Make sure that your test case will make sense to a test participant.

The test participants are the people who are following your instructions.

- They tend to be quite literal, and nervous, so you cannot leave any steps out, or "assume" that they know how to do something.

- They want to see if the new functionality works for them.

- They have an investment in making sure that the software does what it is supposed to.

- Because they represent a crowd of other users, the testers tend to be very conscientious in pointing out errors, and areas that are confusing (for example, weak spots in the interface).

Make sure your test cases will help the developers.

Developers review the test cases before you use them, and after the tests, developers rely on the filled-in test cases to prepare a list of defects to be fixed.

For the developers, you have to make sure you are really testing each possible situation. (You hope that your scenarios identified all of these, but as you write, you may discover that there are some error conditions that nobody thought of).

For the project managers (or whoever has to negotiate with the customer representatives and stakeholders), you may need to list the relevant functional requirements statements, or change requests. You are helping them demonstrate to the customers that, hey, we are doing what you asked for here. This kind of traceability is a way of proving that your team has met this small part of the implied contract.

Writing a test case is an act of imagination.

You have to imagine all the ways that the system can fail. What? Software can break?

When thinking about your test cases, recognize that you must really test the functionality of the emerging product. To get in the mood, you might recall situations where software refuses to do what you thought it should.

- You sign into a familiar site, but it offers a hearty welcome to someone else. The login and password tables have gotten corrupted. In apology, the site also says: "Not you? Click here."

- You add one more picture to a giant Word file, and the software crashes. You relaunch, and Word displays the file as it was half an hour ago…the last time that you saved. All else is lost. Do you feel like sending in another report to Microsoft?

- You have set up a half dozen tabs to open in your browser on startup. But the browser does not open any of those tabs. So you close it, and reopen it…and there it goes, opening those tabs. A browser bug? Or user error?

- You fill out all the fields when checking out at an ecommerce site. But you fail to indicate that your credit card is Visa, not MasterCard, the default. So when you submit, the system rejects you, and erases everything you entered. Bad user!

These situations reflect poor design decisions, poor coding, or just plain lack of imagination on the part of the development team.

But now you work with a development team. They have been laboring for weeks to meet the functional requirements you wrote up in the use cases. Now they are ready to see what happens when users try out the new functionality.

What could possibly go wrong?

Later, when we write a procedure for the user, we will act as if everything will go well—and it usually does. Then.

But right now, the system is in development. There are already known bugs, there are unknown bugs, and there are subtle catastrophes waiting to emerge. As writers, we cannot assume that anything is going to work.

In fact, our job is to invent situations that test each function that the programmers have created. Does it work right? Does it fail? Does it work half right, but with the wrong data?

Normally, in the first test, a few things work fine, but a problem arises at step 3, preventing the test participants from continuing.

When a problem arises, the programmers ask: How did this happen? They need to know exactly what text the user typed, what buttons the user pushed, in what order, and exactly when the blue screen of death appeared.

That information helps them reproduce the bug. If they can "cause" the error repeatedly, they can tinker and tease and tweak, until they catch the problem, and solve it.

Without reproducibility, a bug cannot be fixed.

But to be able to tell the programmers exactly what the test participant was doing, we need to guide that test participant with a very firm hand. Do exactly what I tell you to, and nothing else.

We cannot give them leeway to type any darn thing they feel like. We cannot say, "Oh, just pick an option, any option." We must specify exactly what they should do, completely, no exceptions, no gaps.

Only in the way does the test participant create a trail of clicks, taps, and actions that a programmer can follow, repeating the sequence of actions that precipitate the crash.

Imagine, at every turn, a bug.

Never assume that anything works.

Question the system.

Here's a common function that we need to test: Will the system recognize the user on login?

- To test this, we must set up a dummy account with a particular username and password—before the test.
- Then, in the test, we tell the test participant to login with that particular username and password. The system then goes out to the login and password database, looks up the combination, and decides yay or nay to let the user in. If the user gets locked out, the programmers are going to check the journaling, to make sure the user typed the right stuff. If so, the programmers ask themselves: did we send that correctly to the database? Was our query well formed? Did the database choke on a capital letter?
- We keep control over the test by setting up the preconditions, that is, the dummy username and password.

Question the data.

Here's another question we might want to test: Will the system pull up the correct transactions for the right user during the chosen billing period?

> To test this, we have to set up specific transactions in the dummy account, as preconditions. Let's say we set up these three

transactions, and only these transactions, for the month of April, 2016:

- 4/15/2016 Alarm City, Merchant 4356, (800) 999-7878, $47.67
- 4/16/2016 International House of Wicker, Merchant 98789, (800) 555-8766, $456.76
- 4/16/2016 Target, Merchant 56789, (800) 444-6754, $45.67

Before the test, we have the technicians work inside the system to set up those transactions and tie them to the user account.

Then we ask the test participant, logged in as that user, to call up a statement for April. It should show all three of these transactions, verbatim, and no other transactions. We ask the test participant to check the date, merchant name, merchant number, phone number, and amount, for each transaction.

So we write those details twice—one when we set up preconditions for the test, saying what the technicians need to do to get ready for the test, and again, when we tell the test participant exactly what results to expect when they bring up the statement for April 2016.

With these specifics, we can prove that, yes, the system is in fact pulling up the right data—or not.

But if we had just said that some transactions, undefined, appear, the test participant could say, well, yes, there are some transactions here, so, yes, pass. But we would never know if the right transactions appeared, in the right order, with no extraneous ones in the list.

Running a test

You may want to run a dress rehearsal a day or so in advance of the full testing.

Try your test cases out on one or two people up front. You want to make sure that:

- You have written the scenario and tasks in a way that the users can actually understand and act on. (You can't count on "helping" someone understand later, because that "help" often guides the user in "the right direction," skewing your results.)

- You have prepared the printed or onscreen version of the scenario, the tasks, and consent forms.
- Your product or site is ready to be tested on these computers, in this room, at this time of day.
- Your estimate of the time each task will take is, more or less, accurate.
- You have payment ready, if you are paying participants, or gifts to show your appreciation.

Be methodical about your preparations before the test.

- Make sure you have enough copies of all materials.
- Check all equipment to make sure it is working.
- Make sure the coffee and tea are hot, and the bagels and chocolates are fresh.
- Welcome each person individually, introduce yourself if necessary, and get them to calm down.

Be there.

You learn an enormous amount just by watching what a participant is doing.

- When the participant begins the test, withdraw behind or to the side, and observe, without talking, intervening, or yawning.
- Record your observations quietly in a printed copy of your test case.

In their book on Design Guidelines (1982), Joe Meyers and Bruce Tognazzini made the case for being right there, watching one user at a time:

- "Ninety-five percent of the stumbling blocks are found by watching the body language of the users. Watch for squinting eyes, hunched shoulders, shaking heads, and deep, heart-felt sighs.
- "When a user hits a snag, he will assume it is 'on account of he is not too bright': he will not report it; he will hide it ...
- "Do not make assumptions about why a user became confused. Ask him. You will often be surprised to learn what the user thought the program was doing at the time he got lost."

Yes, management often argues that you should just send users off on their own to run the tests, and call in their comments. This "unmoderated" testing can alert you to major problems, but because you cannot watch participants and talk with them during and after the test, you miss invaluable observations and insights.

Beware of the temptations...

- To defend your work
- To give answers and overlook the fact that the user had a problem with the documentation or product
- To shame the user
- To ignore what the user is doing, moment to moment
- To wince or cry out when the user makes an error
- To crowd the room with participants, and hope you can learn something from their debriefings, at the end. (Waste of time).

Keep your hands off!

Leave participants to suffer until they give up, or you can't stand their pain any more. Wait before intervening. If possible, wait until the user asks for help.

Don't rush. You know this material, but they do not. Give participants time to complete their work.

If you sense that a participant is confused, or blocked, ask.

Keep your shock and surprise under control.

If the participant looks surprised, ask, after a pause, "Is this what you expected?" Find out what they thought would happen, and see how that differs from what they see in front of them.

Be a Rogerian therapist: Repeat what they said, to make sure you really understand it, and to avoid leading. (Carl Rogers pioneered this approach to psychotherapy).

Avoid cuing, such as:

- "Any idiot off the street can use this. Why are you having trouble?"
- "How did that happen?"
- "Where the heck are you?"

Try to understand what it looks like inside their head.

Do not canvas for solutions. Participants can tell you where they got in trouble. But beware of the Helpful Harry who offers various fixes. You are looking for problems, not solutions.

Only intervene when disaster strikes.

Here are some circumstances in which you must intervene:

- The system crashes.
- A bug makes such a mess out of the software that you must reinstall and reboot.
- You realize that the documentation has given the wrong directions, and the participant is now completely stuck.
- You see that the user will never, ever, complete the task. (Recover and move to the next task).

While repairing the damage, and restarting, learn from the participants:

- What were they thinking, and feeling?
- How did they react to this or that part of the interface?

Watch for usability problems as you test

Usability testing is part of rapid development; it is not quality control.

The point is to find out what works and what does not, and make improvements.

We do not test every button, command, and dialog box, as quality control must.

We are primarily interested in the user's internal experience, conceptual modeling, anxieties, confusion—not whether the product works the way the specs say it should.

We have already debated many of the issues we want resolved; we are on the alert for evidence pointing toward one or another solution. We are not neutral scientists; we are members of the development team looking for what works for our audience.

Debrief on both function and usability issues.

After the test is over, and the participant has filled out any post-test questionnaires you have, offer a refill on that coffee, and chat.

Begin with very open-ended questions:
- So what do you think?
- How did it go?
- What's your general impression?

Move through each task, asking questions such as:
- What did you expect to happen?
- Did that happen?
- Was there something you found confusing here?

After giving the participant time to recollect freely, focus on any area in which the participant seemed to have trouble.

Write up defects and new requests

A defect is a sign that the system is not performing to spec.

You may not know the cause. But you can report the symptom.

A defect causes the software to fail to meet requirements, in some way.

Your job is to do some preliminary analysis of the nature of each defect.

The formality of your report on defects depends on the complexity of the project, and the size of your team.

On a small team, with the developers present, you may merely need to make a list of problems to be fixed, more as a reminder than a metric.

On a big team, with a complicated project, you may need to enter defects into a database, or a spreadsheet.

Distinguish between a defect and a change request.

If something is wrong, it is a defect.

If the user gets an idea for a really neat new feature, that is a change request.

Change requests go into their own hopper.

In a defect report, you focus on problems with the code that implements existing requirements, only.

Analyze each defect.

To help the development team discuss the defects, you need to write them up in a methodical way. Here are some standard fields for your report, or database.

Discovered By

Name of the person who did the testing.

Test Date

Important, because later the developers will need to check that they fixed the bug **after** this date, and there are no reports of a similar defect after their fix.

Test Case or Use Case Scenario Number

So the developers can look up the context.

Defect Type

Incomplete

- Is something missing? (A field, a form, a button, for example). Then the defect indicates something is incomplete.
- Is something only there in draft, or as a shell, so it is not yet complete?

Incorrect

- Is the result of a calculation wrong?
- Does the wrong data show up?
- Does the process not follow the one described in the requirements?

Inconsistent

- Do two elements of the same kind look different, without a customer request that they look different?
- Are the same processes or data presented or formatted in different ways without any customer requirement to do so?
- Does one element duplicate another, unnecessarily?

6. Creating a test case

Defect Severity

Failure

The system crashes, or the data is lost.

Functional

The wrong content appears, or the functionality is incorrect, producing the wrong answer, say. Links go to the wrong locations.

Aesthetic

The interface looks ugly. Buttons overlap, a table does not fit on the printed page.

Usability

The interface confused the user. The navigation was unclear. The user made numerous mistakes, attributable to misleading screen design, poor menus, ambiguous links. The user had trouble backing out of bad choices, or recovering from errors.

Cost to Repair

You may leave this blank, for the developers to fill in later.

Disposition

You may leave this blank, for the developers to fill in later.

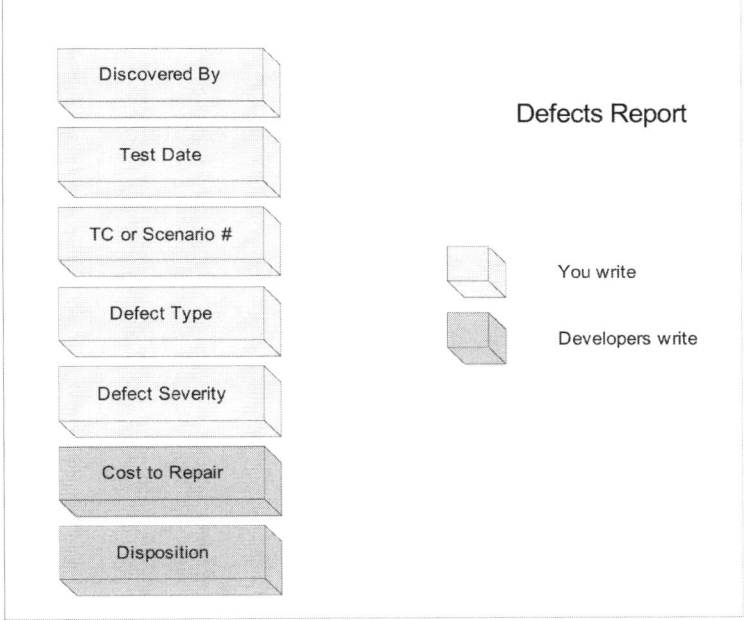

Prioritizing and fixing the worst bugs

The team reviews the problems that have been discovered in testing, and decides what to do about them.

- Some bugs are trivial. They can easily be fixed, but they do not make much difference.
- Some bugs, the worst kind, are intermittent. They come up now and then. The team cannot reproduce them. The problems go away for a while, then reappear. These bugs may never be fixed.
- Some bugs reduce or break key functionality. They must be fixed before you can ship the product.

As the engineers work on fixing the most serious problems, they may ask you to write several new test cases centering on these functions, to try out different possible setups, or paths through the procedure.

So you write new variations on your original test case, and then you watch as a new bunch of test participants work through these, step by step.

With a little luck, the testing comes out successful after only one or two iterations. Without that luck, you may be running the same tests five or six times, as the engineers keep patching and repairing and refactoring.

Some thoughts on testing

"If you don't like testing your product, your customers won't like it either." — Anonymous

"The trouble with programmers is that you can never tell what a programmer is doing until it's too late." —Seymour Cray

"Talk is cheap. Show me the code." —Linus Torvalds

"Optimism is an occupational hazard of programming; feedback is the treatment." —Kent Beck

"Without requirements or design, programming is the art of adding bugs to an empty text file." —Louis Srygley

"Where is the 'any' key?" — Homer Simpson

"All code is guilty, until proven innocent." – Anonymous

"A bug in the hand is worth two in the box." – Anonymous

"Testing is an infinite process of comparing the invisible to the ambiguous in order to avoid the unthinkable happening to the anonymous." – James Bach

Chapter 7. About user stories

For some projects, developing a set of use cases can be overkill. For short, small projects, particularly business applications that face a rapidly changing environment, you may do better to work with user stories.

A user story describes in one sentence what the user wants from the system, and why.

The user story is not a requirement. It's a jumping-off point. It springs from a discussion, and serves as the basis for further discussions, and somewhere in all that talk, the actual requirements emerge.

One user story, then, serves as a focal point for an extended conversation between the developers and the folks who represent the people who will use their work—the users.

And a collection of user stories can provide a helpful agenda for many more conversations, keeping an agile project as a whole on track, moving toward all the users' goals.

Ultimately, a collection of user stories provides a team with a set of functional requirements, more loosely defined than with use cases, but more agile, flexible, and quick. Like use cases, user stories answer key questions for both the customer and the development team: what functions must be built, for whom, and how can we tell that we have succeeded?

User stories also answer at least one more question: Why? Why does the actor have this goal? What is its value, or benefit to this person? In this way, user stories always assume a human actor, where use cases can sometimes exist with a non-human actor, such as a sensor, database, or network.

And user stories shift the focus away from writing documents that act as contracts. Instead, user stories aim to provoke discussions that lead to mutual understanding, as a jump-off point for coding.

In this chapter, we'll take a quick look at the way user stories provide a team with more—and less—than use cases.

What is a user story?

One sentence. (Often written on a yellow sticky or a note card).

A user story has a very simple structure:

As a [role] I want [goal] for [benefits]

"As a <role>, I want <my goal> so that I get this <benefit>."

Examples:

- As a sales person, I want to be able to locate my customers by their first and last names, so I can quickly get to their customer relationship records.

- As a non-administrative user, I want to be able to modify my own schedule, so that I can set up my own appointments.

- As a regular smartphone customer, I want to move a contact into my Favorites list, so I can call that person with one tap.

- As a user closing the application, I want to be prompted to save if I have made any change in my data since the last save, so that I do not lose any of my work.

What makes a good user story?

The story serves the user.

- It's short. It describes only one user goal.

- It's worthwhile. The user gets a real benefit out of the function.

- It keeps the development team focused on the user, not the feature or function.

- It describes a task. Not a system function, but an action that a user wants to perform, to reach a goal, for a specific benefit.

- It offers hooks for automated responses such as chatbots, because the story gives three clues as to what kind of user questions might come up, and through lookups in the glossary or thesaurus, what relevant responses might be.

- It's negotiable. As discussions unfold, the meaning of the story grows, and changes, aligning more and more with user goals.

The story serves the development team.

- It's easy to discuss, so customers can talk at length about the goal, and

7. About user stories

about the potential benefits, clarifying what the function could mean to them.

- It's meaningful. Because it is written in the first person, the story helps us imagine our way into the point of view of these users, grokking their situation, and the reason why they care about this goal.

- It's malleable. You can keep changing the story right up to the point where you assign it to a programmer to code. As you carry on discussions, you clarify what the story means to the user, and that sharpens the point for developers, who begin to ask questions, and learn.

- It's manageable. It's a discrete unit that we can drop into a plan, assign to an individual programmer or small team, and, usually, complete in one iteration. In discussing the story, the developers and customers can come to shared decisions about resource allocation, and we can more easily change course, as the business situation changes. As the project proceeds, new requests can be placed into the product backlog as stories, rather than issues, defects, or new features, so that the product owner can more easily prioritize by customer value.

- It's minimal. The spare simplicity of that one sentence helps us avoid feature creep, where we might keep adding options that few users really need.

- It's loaded. The terms used to describe roles, goals, and benefits turn out to be key concepts that must be defined during discussions, and perhaps even categorized in a taxonomy and thesaurus.

- It's measurable. Through discussions, we can append test criteria that measure our success. And when we ask users to try out the code, they can tell us whether or not they are getting the benefits described, and if not, what would make the software work better for them.

The story also helps other stakeholders discuss the project.

- Even the marketing team can understand the gist of the functionality being requested.

- The training and support teams can organize their tutorials and knowledgebase around the set of user stories.

- Localization teams can use the user story as a shorthand for the documentation needed.

- Managers can prioritize the backlog far more easily with user stories than with old-fashioned functional requirements, or separate flows within individual use cases. User stories mean more to high-level managers.

What makes a bad story?

- A story that fails to promise something of value to the user. (Irrelevant).

- A story that makes sense only to the developers, because it focuses on purely technical issues. (Too much jargon for stakeholders to grasp).

- A story that assumes technology that the team does not possess, or understand. (Too hard to estimate).

- A story that does not point to a user action that the code can implement. (Too vague and amorphous).

- A story that spells out every action the user must take. (Too much detail).

- A story that assumes a particular user interface. (Too early).

- A story that cannot be tested, because it refers to subjective experiences ("easy to use"), undefined criteria ("quickly," or "appropriately"), or impossible standards ("never," "always").

What are the elements in this pattern?

A user story contains three elements, glued together with boilerplate: "As a [Role]…I want [Goal]…so that…[Benefit]"

A **role** is an abstraction, not an individual human being. A type. A job category. A demographic. Ideally, you have already created a persona representing the person who drives a user story.

Like an actor in a use case, the person who fills a role is the person who initiates an interaction, and exchanges data with the system, to achieve the goal. And this person is the one who gets the most benefit out of the actions *implied* in the narrative. (Remember that the user story leaves out the specific actions that the user must take to reach the goal, so the team can fill those in later).

A **goal** is a concrete, measurable result of actions that we will create later, when we code. In a use case, we often put the goal into the title, such as Withdraw Cash, or Transfer Funds. Note that the goal implies actions that are not described in detail, as they would be in a use case. The goal, then, can be thought of as a task that the user wants to accomplish.

In the user story, we are speaking, briefly, for the user. So we need to express the goal in that person's terms, not our own. The point of view is that of the user, not a developer, or outsider.

The **benefit** is the reason why the user might want to achieve the goal. Why bother? What is the value to this user? What's the payoff?

When we need to prioritize certain user stories, we often turn to the benefit as a way to decide how important a story really is, for the user.

The benefit is often something that the implied actions make possible, perhaps an activity that the user wants to do next, or a system state that will help the user meet some job criterion, metric, or performance indicator.

The benefit gives us context. It suggests why this user might want to carry out this task. It shows the meaning behind the stated goal. That turns out to be extremely helpful for programmers when they are deep in the code, trying to make the many small decisions that will ultimately affect the user's experience—and satisfaction.

The user story is kept deliberately thin to provoke discussion.

The user story leaves out what the user must do, and what the system must do in response—the actual steps. The single sentence does not say how we can test the new function to see if it is working right. It ignores metrics, and conditions for success, which we may need to add later, during further discussions.

The very simplicity of the user story forces us to talk. At length. In depth. With both developers and stakeholders.

Through conversation, each user story takes on life and depth. Without the conversation, the story is just a hint.

A bonus: In discussions, it's easy to say an entire story in one breath.

And because each user story is on one note card or sticky, we can easily manipulate a bunch of them, during discussions between the developers and the representatives of the users.

Early in the project we can shuffle all our user stories like playing cards, laying out the whole project on a table or a white board, to see how these different stories fit together, what they have in common, what might be missing, and what the whole product will look like.

To define the functional requirements more precisely, we add acceptance tests or criteria.

On its own, a user story does not define exactly what to build, what exceptions to expect, what options to offer. Such vagueness inspires imagination, but raises a key question in our discussions: How can we tell if we have succeeded in building the user story into the product?

As we learn more about the story, we develop what you might think of as appendices: tests that the code must pass, conditions that must be met.

Like alternative flows in a use case, some tests also lay out options, errors, and possible failures. The team develops the code specifically to pass these tests.

Examples for the user story: As a Student, I want to be able to pay my tuition online, so I am able to register for courses.

- Test with Visa, MasterCard, and American Express.
- Test with Diner's Club.
- Test with good, bad, missing Student ID number.
- Test with expired card.
- Test with different tuition amounts.
- Test to see if registration system recognizes that the student has paid tuition.

So a user story comes trailing tests, which give the developers a lot more guidance on what they must do, to pass.

We may also add acceptance criteria.

These offer even more details on what the system must have done for the user—what we call a post-condition in a use case. So what was removed from sight when we wrote the one-sentence story gets added back in as a kind of addendum.

Examples:

> I know I am done when I see the title of my appointment appear in my calendar, on the right date.

These acceptance criteria are often written down, which means we are creating artifacts that can be tracked, and a way to measure the success or failure of the code. The list of "conditions of success" flesh out the thin user stories, and give them teeth.

Organizing user stories

Even on a small project, with, say, four programmers, the sheer number of user stories can be intimidating. Like a list of requirement statements, the dozens or hundreds of note cards make the mind numb.

To help us make sense of this proliferation of tiny narrative gestures, we need a discussion in which we organize the set of user stories visually.

Remember the way a use case model offered a visual representation of all the proposed use cases, for discussion and scoping, early in the project? We need something similar here, to answer questions about our blizzard of user stories.

Just drafting a long list of user stories is not going to do much good. We have to talk about them. And, to make the discussion productive, we need to see the whole project, really see it, in pieces that we can move around, physically, touching those cards and stickies, and maybe, gasp, even crumpling up some and throwing them away, and adding others. We must interact with a pile of slips of paper.

We need the tangible, visual artifacts right there in front of us, to be able to visualize the whole project, and to swoop down into the smallest possible function, on one particular card. Up and down, zooming in, zooming out, we all can work toward a common vision.

Seeing the big picture

Because each user story on our white board—or the wall, or the floor—describes a single goal, we can sometimes organize several of them into an overall process, where a user moves forward from one goal to another. Perhaps the user is handling an invoice, responding to an emergency travel request, or requesting corrective action after a mishap. Each process involves several activities, each with its own small goal. And generally, we have to do those activities in a standard sequence. Hence, we can sometimes arrange our stickies from left to right, showing the way a user moves forward through that process.

On the analogy of travel, we can look at such a layout as a map. For the stakeholders, such a sequence chimes with their own understanding of their work. ("First I do this, then I have to get this other thing done, and then..."). Not as formal as a diagram of a business process, this set of stories "stands for" that sequence of actions, without reducing it to a series of steps, as in a use case, or expanding it into a complex, hard-to-follow flow chart.

Looking at the map, your stakeholders can spot gaps, stories that need to be inserted, and duplicates that can be removed. And during discussions, you can append, underneath, the alternatives, details, and exceptions that you may need to deal with—the shorter stories.

The more items that you add to a map, the more you approach epic proportions.

When we have a bunch of narrowly focused stories, such as Paying with a MasterCard, Paying with Visa, Paying with Paypal, we may go abstract, and aggregate, to create an overarching story, Paying with a Credit Card. That's an epic.

Or we may have to break apart an epic into its constituent short stories. For example, we may discover that the "user" may actually be several different roles.

> Epic: As a user, I can save a trip, so I can reuse it later.

Decomposing that, we discover new roles:

> As a Premium customer, I can have my trip saved automatically, for future use.

> As a Guest customer, I can choose to set up an account so that my trip details will be saved for future use.

Such shuffling, disassembling, and re-assembling, can help us articulate commonalities, as well as exceptions. If overwhelmed by detail, we can edit the map to focus on particular themes, such as stories common to a particular role, goal, benefit, or object, to single out potential prototypes, or to highlight a minimum viable product. A good question when editing: How can we make our map the right size?

Good news: A map, with or without epics, is rarely as complex and detailed as a full diagram of a complex business process, which may include several dozen nodes, each of which involves several scenarios, plus decision diamonds, footnotes, and exceptions. (For a large project like that, we might prefer to create use case models that point back to a process flow, and a glossary of terms).

User stories take on meaning as they go.

In a fast-changing domain with short release cycles, user stories work well in an Agile, Lean, or Extreme Programming environment, because stories encourage such a conversational, collaborative, and flexible approach to requirements.

In these circumstances, getting working software is more important than documenting everything we do, up front, during, and after the project.

And because user stories encourage discussions that create mutual understanding between customers and developers, they help participants view the process as a collaborative effort, with plenty of give and take, rather than a contract negotiation.

During planning and commitment phases, the team and customers sort through the backlog of stories, to decide what should be done first, based on several questions:

- Which story brings the biggest value to the business?
- Which story involves the biggest risk from a programming point of view (difficult to program, untested tools, undecided impacts)? (Often we choose to do this one first).
- How fast can we complete the code for this story?
- What batch of stories can we finish for the next release?

Because each user story is so narrowly focused, it can usually be developed in one iteration (like a single scenario within a use case). Then we test, to see if developers have really captured what the users want to do. Does this meet your goal? Does it yield the benefits you were after?

When users see the working code, they may like it right away. But more likely, they find some aspects confusing.

- They discover that this functionality is not really what they want.
- They think of five other things they would like, things they did not think of before.
- They ask questions that the developers never thought of.
- They refine their own requirements.
- They help developers get a better sense of what they really need and want.
- They mention edge cases that have never been mentioned before.

Such conversations may lead to new stories, or new understandings of the existing ones. In a waterfall environment, such discoveries provoked anxiety and change notices, leading to delay. But with user stories, change is built into the process, so we can make improvements quickly.

How do user stories compare with use cases?

They're less formal, so they may encourage easier conversations, as the users or their stand-ins explain their needs to the programmers.

They demand less overhead. You rarely need elaborate tracking, detailed version control, or a complex database.

Their small size often means that each story can be thought of as demanding only about one or two weeks of one programmer's time.

Much of the text is **written by the customers**, or recorded by you using the customers' language, so they know what the story means.

What do the two approaches have in common?

Both user stories and use cases aim to clarify communication between stakeholders and developers. Both approaches focus on what the users want and need, in contrast to the artifacts that support the development team, such as entity relationship diagrams, class hierarchies, and constraints imposed by tools or management diktat.

Both approaches define requirements that we call *functional*, because they describe something that the system must do for the user—some functionality we must build. So the user story addresses some of the same questions that we answer in a use case.

Who is the primary **actor**?

> The user story identifies the actor, the person who gets the benefit of all the action, as a *role*.

What is the actor's **goal**?

> Like the *name* of a use case, the sentence describes a goal that has meaning for the user.

What is the **function**?

> Like the *brief description* in a use case, the user story offers a summary description of the key function, but the user story leaves out all step-by-step action.

What's the **context**?

> A user story describes what would be a single *scenario* in a use case, whereas a use case includes all the scenarios. So a user story might be the happy day scenario, or it might be one of the alternative scenarios. Each user story envisions one scenario.

What's the **theme** or **epic**?

> When we put together three or four user stories in a theme, or in an epic, they often add up to the set of scenarios in a single use case, with its Happy Day scenario and its alternative flows.

What **steps** should the user do? And how should the system respond?

> The user story leaves out all user actions, where the use case spells each one out, in detail, and specifies just what the system should do in response. With a use case in hand, we can test how the system is responding to each user action, one step at a time...useful for debugging, and for documenting the material for a user guide. By contrast, the user story waves its hands and tells the programmers, "I am giving you the general idea, but I am leaving the user actions to you to figure out."

What's the **benefit**?

> The user story makes the payoff more visible than a use case, where the result of all the steps is buried at the bottom of the page, as a post condition. The post condition focuses on the system state, not the value to the user. We read it, but ask, why would anyone want that? The Benefit section of a user story gives us a much better sense of the human rationale, the reason why someone might want to do this.

How can users **test** for success?

> We've seen how we can move from a use case to test cases, building on the elaborate detail in the use case, so we can test, and, if necessary, debug, step by step.

> With a user story, we must test by having users try out the new software without standing at their elbow, saying what action to take, and then, and then. We tell them the goal, not the steps. And we observe. If they have difficulty navigating a form, or get into trouble at some stage, we notice that, and decide on the spot how to fix the problem. Less formal, but for a small project, effective.

How long do we **save** the artifact?

> The user story is ephemeral. Quickly written, discussed, and thrown away as a casual work product, the user story does not contain a record of decisions made.

> By contrast, a use case is forever. As a contract between developers and customers it continues to exist as long as the product is being developed, or maintained. How come?

Traceability, responsibility, budgeting, updates, error correction, debugging. On a large project, such as building a ship or satellite, use cases spell out exactly what must be done, and, when that is done, we can go back and see whether or not the product matches the original requirements. On these projects, traceability works better with the atomized use case, where each scenario can be built, tested, and marked done.

But user stories are like notes of a conversation; they lack the details you would need to use, if you wanted to confirm that, yes, we did each step, each system response, correctly. Adding tests or conditions of success may help…and we may want to preserve the tests, if not the stories themselves, for maintenance programmers to use in the future.

How **fast** can we move to code?

User stories save time. You can write a dozen rather general stories to get an overview of the whole project, then focus on a few, fleshing them out by creating more granular stories, as you commit to development. Compare that with the traditional approach of getting all your requirement statements or use cases finalized before writing code.

Yes, we can impose constraints on stories, saying something like, "None of our stories can take more than two weeks to develop." But a use case has no such time constraints.

Also, we usually develop the code for a user story in one iteration, where work on a use case may be divided into several phases, as the team shifts focus from the Happy Day scenario to the alternative flows.

How **big** is the project?

User stories work best on Agile, Lean, and Extreme Programming projects, with a small team and budget, where each iteration delivers working software within two to four weeks. User stories make it easy to reprioritize every few weeks, as goals fluctuate

The more complex the project, the more we turn to use cases. They help us deal with business domains that involve a multiplicity of roles, alternative flows, exceptions, options, external regulations, contractual obligations, and organizational conflicts.

Up front, use cases can act as contractual agreements, blueprints for development, and focal points for discussion, though those meetings tend to be more formal than in an Agile world. As content, a use case can flow easily into a set of user test cases,

7. About user stories

and procedures in user documentation. Throughout the project, use cases can provide a linch-pin when we are bringing together large development teams and diffuse groups of stakeholders. The bigger the budget, and the longer the schedule, the more we must rely on use cases for project memory, traceability, and proof of success.

Choosing a path

This book is about use cases, not user stories. But in this little chapter, we have seen a few of the ways that user stories compare with use cases. In gathering requirements, it seems, we keep trying to do a better job in matching user expectations, wishes, and goals. And when we fail, we innovate, develop hybrid approaches to requirements, cheat, struggle, and create our own variations on these patterns.

Nothing's fixed. The process we work in has often been overdetermined by our organization's culture, tools, customers, market challenges, past successes and failures. Each of us must navigate our own way forward, picking what we think works best in our own environment. Teams customize hybrid and jury-rigged processes as often as they cobble together new tools.

So one size does not fit all. When the project's small, user stories may be an adroit way to gather and track requirements. But when the project gets complex, we may turn toward use cases. Neither approach is perfect. Our job is to adapt.

Write a Use Case

Appendix: Nonfunctional requirements

We've been looking at functional requirements—specs that describe a user goal, and the functions that support that goal. But a development team must satisfy other requirements, ones that apply to the whole development process, and the standards or rules that apply to the entire program, not a particular use case or user story. "Nonfunctional" is a weird name for these requirements, because, after all, they must work.

A nonfunctional requirement is a real requirement.

- You must be able to verify that you have met the condition.
- You may have to rewrite to make the requirement testable.
- If something cannot be measured or observed, perhaps it is an intent, or a general goal, not a requirement.

We do not usually include these "nonfunctional" requirements in the use cases. (Use cases focus on *functional* requirements).

Some nonfunctional requirements specify operating systems the application must work on, laws and regulations that the application must comply with, design constraints, such as a programming framework that must be used to develop the product, and the URPS—Usability, Reliability, Performance, Supportability. Let's look at some of these, to get a more granular picture of the extent of nonfunctional requirements.

Usability

Areas

- Human factors
- Esthetics
- Consistency
- Documentation

Examples of testable requirements

- Training time requirements
- Measurable task times
- User abilities

- Conformity with standards

Reliability

Areas

- Frequency or severity of failure
- Recoverability
- Predictability
- Accuracy

Examples of testable requirements:

- Availability x% of a test week.
- Accuracy.
- Hours between failure.
- Maximum bugs per thousand lines of code (KLOC)

Performance

Areas

- Speed
- Efficiency
- Resource usage
- Throughput
- Response time

Examples of testable requirements

- Measure the speed or efficiency of the system in operation
- Capacity
- Throughput
- Response time
- Memory
- Use of scarce resources

Supportability

Areas

- Testability
- Extensibility
- Adaptability
- Maintainability
- Compatibility
- Configurability
- Serviceability
- Installability
- Localizability
- Robustness

Examples of testable requirements

- Specific languages, tools, DBMS
- Installation procedures
- Error handling standards
- Reporting standards

Design constraints

What goes into design constraints?

A design constraint is a limitation on the way the system is designed, or the process used to build the system.

We do not handle design constraints in a use case.

A design constraint affects the way the application is designed and developed:

- The programming environment or framework
- The programming languages used
- The tools used in the process
- The standards that the application must meet

Examples of design constraints:

- The system must operate on the existing SQL Server farm.
- The team will use J2EE in development.
- The corporate logo must appear on every screen.

Resources

Beyer, H. and K. Holtzblatt. 1997. *Contextual Design: Defining Customer-Centered Systems*. Morgan Kauffman.

Bittner, Kurt, and Ian Spence. 2003. *Use Case Modeling*. Addison-Wesley.

Booch, Grady, James Rumbaugh, and Ivar Jacobson. 2005. *The Unified Modeling Language User Guide*. Addison-Wesley.

Cockburn, Alistair. 2000. *Writing Effective Use Cases*. Addison-Wesley.

Cohn, Mike. 2004. *User Stories Applied*. Addison-Wesley.

Constantine, Larry, and Lucy A. D. Lockwood. 1999. *Software for Use: A Practical Guide to the Models and Methods of Usage-Centered Design*. Addison-Wesley.

Gottesdiener, Ellen. 2002. *Requirements by Collaboration*. Addison-Wesley.

IBM REQ 480 *Mastering Requirements Management with Use Cases, Student Manual*. IBM.

Jacobson, Ivar, Magnus Christenson, Patrik Jonsson, and Gunnar Overgaard. 1992. *Object-Oriented Software Engineering: A Use-Case Driven Approach*. ACM Press.

Jacobson, Ivar, Maria Ericsson, and Agneta Jacobson. 1995. *The Object Advantage*. ACM Press.

Patton, Jeff, with Peter Economy. 2014. *User Story Mapping: Discover the Whole Story, Build the Right Product*. O'Reilly.

Price, Jonathan Reeve. *Get Past the Tags: How to Write (and Read) XML*. 2019. Communication Circle.

Royce, Walker. 1998. *Software Project Management: A Unified Framework*. Addison-Wesley.

Author's Note

Q: How did you get into writing about use cases?

I regularly work as a writer and consultant in high-tech environments, gathering requirements for hardware and software projects. My clients include an A to Z of computer companies, national laboratories, and universities. I coach writers, business analysts, and developers as we build use cases, test cases, procedures, user stories, training materials, and information architectures.

Q: What's your background?

I was a Latin major at Harvard, but when I discovered that I had run out of undergraduate courses, and might have to learn Greek, I backed out, and became an English major. I went to the Yale School of Drama as a playwright, and earned a Doctorate of Fine Arts, writing about Shakespeare's *King John* over in the English Department. I taught drama for two years at New York University, but quit to write full time.

In New York, I wrote articles for magazines like *Harper's, Reader's Digest*, and *TV Guide*. I co-authored a book on drama with John Lahr—*Life Show: How to See Theater in Life and Life in Theater*. And in other books (and a bunch of articles) I explored video art and TV commercials. At the same time, I was doing conceptual and video art in West Broadway Gallery, and concrete poetry wherever.

To make a little more money, I ran the Shakespeare Institute, a summer graduate program for teachers at the University of Bridgeport, and then taught at Rutgers. But when I heard that there was life west of the Hudson, I moved to California, where I discovered technical writing.

I spent four years as a Senior Technical Writer at Apple Computer, which was a little like being in graduate school: lots of intense, very bright people obsessing about obscure subjects (like laser printers, Chinese fonts, hypertext, and operating systems). I wrote a styleguide for the technical writers, called *How to Write an Apple Manual*, which morphed into *How to Write a Computer Manual*, which became, with the help of Henry Korman, Mick Renner, Linda Urban, and Adam Rochmes, *How to Communicate Technical Information*.

After graduating from Apple, I wrote a lot of help systems, and consulted with a wide range of high-tech firms on customer assistance, first within apps, then in the cloud. Along the way, I've gathered functional requirements for small, medium, and large projects in high tech corporations and national labs.

And through workshops and online classes at universities such as the University of California Extension at Santa Cruz, I've trained more than a thousand writers, business analysts, and programmers in crafting use cases, test cases, user stories, and good old-fashioned task topics.

The folks I've worked with have all contributed to this book. They asked questions, and I've added the answers. They talked about what made requirements useful for developers, and they shared horror stories of projects that failed because of requirements that were inconsistent, incomplete, inaccurate, ambiguous, or worse. Together, we learned to avoid most of these pitfalls, while serving both stakeholders and the development team.

My wife Lisa and I have also published *Hot Text: Web Writing that Works*, a book on how to write effectively for the Web. In my spare time, I create digital art that appears online and in galleries and museums.

Q: What other books have you published recently?

- *Get Past the Tags: How to Write (and Read) XML*
- *American Scenery: Thomas Cole vs NASA*
- *Remapping Paris*
- *The Liquid Border: The Rio Grande from El Paso to the Gulf of Mexico*

Q: Where can we go for more info?

- Blog: http://museumzero.blogspot.com/
- Linked In: http://www.linkedin.com/in/JonathanReevePrice
- Amazon Author Page: https://www.amazon.com/author/jonathanprice
- Www.webwritingthatworks.com
- MuseumZero.Art
- JonathanReevePrice at gmail

Q: Where do you live, anyway?

Lisa and I live in a small house overlooking the Rio Grande River, where it flows through New Mexico on its way to Texas and Mexico. We have two sons, Ben and Noah, who live near us. Our Corgi dogs, Sterling and Jagger, run and bark to chase away hot air balloons.

Index

A

Activity diagram 108-111

Actors
- Definition 83
- Described in third person 72
- Examples 62, 68, 83, 126
- Goals of 45-46, 83
- In procedures 72
- In relation to function 44
- In test cases 137, 160-161
- In use-case models 43-45, 51-53, 83
- In use cases 65-66, 130-131
- Listing 83
- Naming 43-45, 83-84
- Organizing around 53-54
- Primary 83-84
- Purpose 79
- Systems as 52-53, 83
- User story and 196
- Vision document 83

Agile
- Small projects 2
- Use cases and 2
- User stories and 194-195, 198

Alternate flows
- Alternative scenarios 89-91
- Benefits 90
- Criteria 89-91, 101-103, 133
- Definition 76, 89, 101-102
- Examples 64, 70, 89, 101-103, 128-129
- Instead of conditions 103
- Listing 101-103
- Repetitions 103
- Section 101

Apple 206

Artifacts
- Feature list 2-3
- Requirement statements 2, 3
- Stakeholder needs 2
- Use cases 2, 3
- User stories 2, 3

Audiences

Development team 1, 41, 66-67, 72-74, 76, 85, 87-88, 90, 93, 136, 145-149, 153-157, 159, 161, 164-169, 171, 172, 174, 176, 183-185, 189-192, 195-197, 206
Discussing use cases 67
For functional requirements 1, 2
For procedures 72-74
For test cases 135-136
For user stories 187-190
Stakeholders iii-iv, 1-2, 4-5, 40-41, 53, 61, 66-67, 73-74, 90, 93, 134, 176, 193
Test cases and 135-136, 145-149, 153-157, 159, 161, 164-169, 171, 172, 174, 176, 183-185
Use cases 41, 67, 72-74, 76, 85, 87-88, 90, 93, 196-197
User stories 188-192, 195

B

Bach, James 186
Basic flow
    Checklist 132-133
    Columns 92-98
    Definition 92
    Elements in 78, 92-98
    Examples 63-64, 69, 92-98, 127
    Interactions in 92-97
    Sequence of events 75
    System responses 92-97
    Triggering 98
    User actions 92-96
Beck, Kent 186
Beyer, H 205
Bittner, Kurt 205
Booch, Grady 205
Brief descriptions
    Content 81, 130
    Examples 55-57, 68, 81-82, 126
Business domain 12, 16
Business model 15
Business rules 85, 131, 159

C

Change requests 85
Christenson, Magnus 205
Cockburn, Alistair 62, 205
Code
    Identifier (ID) 29, 40, 75, 130, 137, 159
    Writing code 2-3, 5, 32, 40, 60, 61, 74, 106, 133, 143, 155, 157, 186, 202

Index

Cohn, Mike 205
Constantine, Larry 205
Contextual Design 205
Conversations
    Use cases and 5-7, 41
    User stories and 187-191, 193-194, 195, 198
    Vision document and 23
    Writer's role in iv
Constraints
    Design 27-28
    In Vision document 24
    Statements of 28
    Types 24
Cray, Seymour 186

D

Database
    Actor 43, 52-53, 62, 187
    Alternative flows and 101
    Defects 183-184
    Preconditions 63, 162-163, 178
    Queries 136, 171, 178
    Requirements statements in 29, 34, 36-37
    Scenarios and 89
    Stakeholder requests 13
    Steps and 113, 171
    Traceability and 26, 34, 36-37, 86, 196
    Tracking Vision ideas 26
    Use case model and 43, 52-53
Developers
    As audience for requirements 1, 4, 41, 66-67, 72-74, 76, 85, 87-88, 90, 93, 136, 145-149, 153-157, 159, 161, 164-169, 171, 172, 174, 176, 183-185, 189-192, 195-197, 206
    Priorities 9
    Reviewing statements 34-38
    Testing 135-136, 145-147, 155, 183, 186
    User stories 189, 190-192, 195, 198
    Using preconditions 87-88
    Writing code 2-3, 5, 32, 40, 60, 61, 74, 106, 133, 143, 155, 157, 186, 202
Diagram
    Activity 108
    Checklist 134
    Decisions 109, 111
    Elements 108-111
    Examples 71, 108-111, 126

Flow 76, 109
Systems 110-111
Documentation plan 25
Domain model
Cardinality and 16
Defined 16
Relationships in 16
Terms in glossary 16
Vision document and 16

E

Economy, Peter 205
Epic 194, 197
Ericsson, Maria 205
Extension Points
Definition 76, 104
Examples 70, 104-105
Format 104
Section 104-105
Extreme Programming 194-195, 198

F

Feature
Attributes 25
Baseline set 20
Brainstorming for 18
Classifying 19
Definition 18
Examples 18, 121
Identifying 18-20
List 2-3
Naming 19
Needs and 17, 18
Not requirements 20
Prioritizing 19-20, 24
Requested 26
System perspective and 18
Test cases and 159
Traced in database 26
Use cases and 85-86, 122, 131
Vision document and 18-20
Fowler, Martin 62
Function
Described step by step 3, 4, 66
In requirement statements 41
Requirement 1
Task 1, 3, 4

Index

           User story and 196
    Functional requirements
           Definition 1, 2, 27
           Examples 122-124
           Scope 21
           Statements as 27, 41-42, 85
           Test cases and 159
           Use cases as 27, 41-42, 72-74, 131
           User stories and 187-189

G

    Goals
           Examples 47-51
           Features and 46
           Of actors in use-case models 45-46, 57
           Reflecting in use case name 45-46, 49, 50, 57, 79
           Testing with 155
           User actions and 47
           User stories 196
    Glossary
           Domain model and 16
           Example 125
           Form details 113
           Requirements statements and 33
           Vision document 15
    Gottesdiener, Ellen 205

H

Harper's Magazine 206
Harvard 206
Holtzblatt, K. 205
Hot Text: Web Writing that Works (book) 206-207
How to Communicate Technical Information (book) 206
How to Write an Apple Manual (book) 206

I

Identifier (ID) 29, 40, 75, 130, 137, 159
IBM 205
IEEE standard 158

J

Jacobson, Agneta 205
Jacobson, Ivar 61-62, 205
Jagger 207
Jonsson, Patrik 205

K

Korman, Henry 206

L
Lahr, John 206
Lean Programming 194-195, 198
Life Show (book) 206
Lockwood, Lucy A.D. 205

M
Map 193-194

N
Name
    Actor's point of view 45-46, 79
    Criteria for 49, 57, 79, 130
    Describes goal 45-46, 50, 75, 79
    Examples 45, 49-52, 62, 68, 71, 79
    Moving from use case model 78
    Position in use case 77
    Suggests user action 49

Needs
    Defined 10
    Examples 10, 118-120
    Identifying 9-13
    Requests 10, 12-13, 18, 20, 23, 26, 37, 39, 118
    Stakeholders 2, 9-13, 23, 118-120
    Test cases and 159
    Traced in database 26
    Translated into features 2, 5-6, 18-20

New York University 206
Nielsen, Jakob 153
NN Group 155
Nonfunctional requirements 201-204
    Definition 201
    Design constraints 203-204
    Performance 202
    Reliability 202
    Supportability 203
    Usability 201-202
    Use cases and 201

O
Object Advantage (book) 205
Object-Oriented Programming
    Jacobson, Ivar 61-62
    Object-Oriented Software Engineering (book) 62
    The Object Advantage (book) 62
    Use cases and 61-62

Object-Oriented Software Engineering (book) 205
Overgaard, Gunnar 205

P

Pareto Principle 16
Patton, Jeff 205
Post conditions
    Checklist 134
    Defined 67, 76, 106
    Examples 64, 70, 106-107, 129
    Guaranteed 106
    Observable result 106
    System state 72, 75, 106-107
Preconditions
    Checklist 132
    Defined 67, 87
    Examples 63, 68, 87-88, 126
    In test cases 137-138, 160-163
    System state 72, 75, 87
Price, Ben 207
Price, Jonathan
    Amazon 207
    American Scenery: Thomas Cole vs NASA (book) 207
    Background 206-207
    Blog 207
    Get Past the Tags (book) 205
    Hot Text: Web Writing that Works (book) 206-207
    How to Communicate Technical Information (book) 206
    How to Write an Apple Manual (book) 206
    Life Show (book) 206
    The Liquid Border (book) 207
    LinkedIn 207
    Remapping Paris (book) 207
    Resources 207
    Websites 207
Price, Lisa 206-207
Price, Noah 207
Priorities 24
Problems
    Analyzing 14-17
    Business model and 15
    Context 15
    Definition model 24
    Root causes 14-15, 17
    Solutions 16-17, 18
    Vision document and 23-24

Procedure
- Compared with use case 72-74
- Purpose 74
- Traced in database 26

Process
- Gathering requirements iv, 1-3, 6-7
- Rational Unified Process (RUP) 5-7, 114, 143

Product
- Defined in Vision Document 3, 9, 22, 24
- Development as process 6-7
- Overview 24
- Positioning 22
- Satisfying needs 2-3

Project
- Complexity 2
- Cost 3
- Failure 1
- Rational Unified Process 5-6
- Scale 2

Q

R

Rational Unified Process (RUP) 5-7, 114, 143
Reader's Digest 206
Renner, Mick 206
Requests 10, 12-13, 18, 20, 21, 23, 26, 37-39, 85, 91, 118, 144
Requirements
- Definition 27
- Derived from 27
- Discussed iii
- Function 1, 3, 4, 41, 66, 196
- Gathering 1
- Non-functional 27, 201-204
- Organization iii
- Section in use case 85-86, 129, 131
- Statements 27-40
- Traced in database 26
- Transformed iii, 4
- Types of 27
- Understood iii, 4
- User goals iii, 4

Requirements by Collaboration (book) 205
Risks
- Ambiguity 4
- Decay 5
- Lack of traceability 5

Index

    Misunderstanding 4
    Navel-gazing 4
    Scope creep 5
    Sprawl 5
    Unresponsiveness 5
Rochmes, Adam 206
Royce, Walker 205
Rumbaugh, James 205

S

Scenarios
    Alternative 89-91
    Architecturally significant 90-91
    Benefits 90
    Content of 131-132
    Definition 90
    Examples 63, 68, 89-91, 126, 137
    Flow of events 75, 89-91
    Parts 89
    Priorities among 91
    User stories and 196
Scope
    In Vision document 21, 24
    System boundaries 21
    Special requirements 75
Shakespeare 206
Simpson, Homer 186
Software for Use (book) 205
Software Project Management (book) 205
Special requirements 75
Spence, Ian 205
Sprints 2
Srygley, Louis 186
Stakeholders
    As audience iii-iv, 1-2, 4-5, 40-41, 53, 61, 66-67, 73-74, 90, 93, 134, 176, 193
    Business domain and 12, 15-16
    Collecting information from 6-7, 9, 12-13, 32, 34, 38, 43, 55, 66-67, 75, 90, 189-191, 196, 199
    Database of requests 13
    Definition 10-11
    Describing 11
    Needs 1-3, 5-6, 9-13, 18, 43, 119-120, 144
    Problems they face 14-17, 18
    Requests 10, 12-13, 18, 20, 21, 23, 26, 37-39, 85, 91, 118, 144
    Requirement statements and 35-37, 41, 131

217

Test cases and 144
Trying out software 2
Use cases and 40-41, 53, 61-62, 66-67, 73-74
User stories and 176, 189-190
Vision document and 23, 28
Wishes 2

Statements
Adjectives and 32
Ambiguity and 35, 39
Approved by stakeholders 4
As functional requirements 2, 3
Audience 3
Checklists 38-40
Clarifying 28-29, 32, 33
Completeness 36, 40
Concision 38
Consistency 35, 38
Correctness 35, 38
Criteria for 35-37
Database and 34
Definition 3, 27-28
Difficult to understand 4
Distinguished from use cases 2, 3
Distinguished from user stories 2,3
Examples 29-31
Functions 3-4, 28, 38
Identifier 29
Interface and 32
List 3
Measurable 31, 32
Modifiable 36, 40
Moving beyond 3
One sentence 29-30
Organization of 40
Number 28
Priorities among 36
Problems with 38, 41
Requirements 27-40
Reviewing 34-37
Set 36-38
Style advice 32-33, 39
System focus 31
Tasks 4
Tests for 34-37
Traceability 36-37, 39
Uniqueness 36, 39

Index

Status
    Verbs in 30-31
    Verifying 35, 39

    Complete 80
    Discovery 80
    Draft 80
    Element in use case 68, 75, 80, 130
    Example 126
    Façade 80
    Filled-in 80
    Focused 80
    Iterations and 80
    Purpose 80

Steps
    Examples 69-70, 127-129
    In test cases 60, 138-142, 156, 163-173
    In use cases 3, 4, 50, 58-59, 60, 65, 66, 72, 75-76, 78, 79, 80, 84, 85, 86, 87, 89-98, 99-103, 104-105, 107, 108, 113, 114, 130, 133-134
    User stories 197

Sterling 207
Subflow
    Against 100
    Checklist 133-134
    Definition 75-76, 99
    Elements 99-100

T

Tag style of use case 114
Tasks 1, 3, 4
Test cases 135-186
    A/B testing 149
    Action in 164-167
    Actors in 137, 160, 164
    Audiences 135-136, 176
    Automated tests 135, 146, 149-150
    Budget 145, 152
    Bugs 143, 146, 176-179, 182-186
    Change requests 183
    Clickstream analysis 149
    Compared with use cases 136, 174-175
    Debriefing after 182-183
    Defects 143, 146, 176-179, 182-186
    Developers and 135-136, 154-155, 157, 176-179
    Dimensions 144-151
    Elements of 158-173
    Example 137-142

219

Expected result in step 167-169
Eye tracking 148
Functional tests 144, 147-150
Heuristic evaluation 151
ID 159
In-person observation 148
Iterative 145
Known bugs 145
Mean time between failures 146
Name 159
Notes 170
Observing 136, 154, 180-182
Participants 135-136, 152-153, 170
Pass/Fail 170
Performance 144, 146
Preconditions in 137, 160-163
Preparations 135, 154-173, 179-180
Protocol analysis 148
Purpose 2, 3, 135-136, 143-145
Quality and 143-151
Rational Unified Process and 143
Related requirements 137, 159
Reliability 144, 146
Remote testing 148-149
Results 142, 167-169
Return on investment 144
Running a test 179-183
Scenarios 156-157, 160
Scheduling 153, 154, 157
Scripts 149-150
Steps 60, 138-142, 163-173
Supportability 144, 147
System test 143
Talk-aloud protocol 148
Tester 170
Traced in database 26
Usability tests 144, 150-151, 155-156
Users 152-153
Validation 143

Torvalds, Linus 186
Traceability
Lack of 5
Requirement statements 36-37, 39
Test cases 176
Use cases and 5, 86, 198-199
Useful in updating 5

Index

User stories and 198

TV Guide 206

U

Unified Modeling Language (UML) 62, 205
University of California 206
Urban, Linda 206
Usability.gov 114-117
Use case 61-134
    Actions in 65, 92-98, 113
    Actor 43-45, 51-53, 65, 68, 75
    Artifacts related to 73
    As artifact 2, 3, 4
    As contract 4
    As standard 6
    Audiences for 41, 72-74, 76, 85, 87-88, 90, 93, 196-197
    Benefits 66-67
    Brief description 68, 75
    Business rules 75, 85
    Change requests 85
    Characteristics 5, 65-67
    Compared to procedure 72-74
    Compared to requirement statements 61
    Defined 4, 61, 65
    Discussed 5, 67, 75
    Elements 75-78
    Examples 62-64, 68-71, 126-129
    Functional decomposition and 58-60
    Functional requirements and 41-42, 46, 65-67
    Goal 4, 45-51, 57, 65-66
    ID 75
    Jacobson, Ivar 61-62
    Name 45-46, 49, 50, 57
    Object-oriented programming and 61-62
    Organizing 77, 112-117
    Other approaches 114-117
    Purpose 74
    Related to test case 73
    Requirements section 85-86
    RUP and 6, 114
    Special requirements 75, 86
    Status 68, 75, 80
    Steps 3, 4, 50, 58-59, 60, 65, 66, 72, 75-76, 78, 79, 80, 84, 85, 86, 87, 89-98, 99-103, 104-105, 107, 108, 113, 114, 130, 133-134
    System response 65-66, 67, 92-98

　　　　　　　　Traced in database 26
　　　　　　　　Triggering 98
　　　　　　　　Understood 5, 66
　　　　　　　　Value 65-66, 113
　　　　　　　　Writing Effective Use Cases (book) 62
Use case model 41-61
　　　　　　　　Actors in 43-45, 51-53
　　　　　　　　Audiences 53-54
　　　　　　　　Brief descriptions 55-57
　　　　　　　　Completeness 58
　　　　　　　　Contents 42-57
　　　　　　　　Definition 42-43
　　　　　　　　Efficiency of 58
　　　　　　　　Functional decomposition and 58-60
　　　　　　　　Goal 45-51
　　　　　　　　Levels in 58
　　　　　　　　Measurable results 58
　　　　　　　　Naming use cases 45-46, 49, 50, 57
　　　　　　　　Organizing 53-54
　　　　　　　　Ovals in 47-51
　　　　　　　　Packages 53-54, 57
　　　　　　　　Purpose 43
　　　　　　　　Reviewing 57-60
　　　　　　　　Systems in 52-53
　　　　　　　　Understandable 57
Use Case Modeling (book) 205
User interface
　　　　　　　　Ignored in use case 72-73, 112
　　　　　　　　Included in procedure 72
Users
　　　　　　　　As audience 41, 72-74
　　　　　　　　Giving feedback 4
　　　　　　　　Goals 4 45-51, 57, 79, 155, 196
　　　　　　　　Needs 1-4, 6, 9-13
　　　　　　　　Participation of 6, 152-153
　　　　　　　　Profile 152
　　　　　　　　Satisfaction 5-6, 66
　　　　　　　　Testing with 152-153
　　　　　　　　Understanding requirements 6
　　　　　　　　Work situation 6
User stories
　　　　　　　　Acceptance criteria 192
　　　　　　　　Actor 196
　　　　　　　　Agile and 194-195, 198
　　　　　　　　Artifacts 2, 3, 193-194, 197-198
　　　　　　　　Audiences 188-192, 195

Basis for conversation 187-191, 193-194, 195, 198
Benefit as element 188, 190-191
Benefits of 187-191, 193-195, 196-199
Compared with use cases 196-199
Criteria for 188-190
Decomposing 194
Definition 187-188
Elements 190-191
Epic 194, 197
Examples 188
Extreme Programming and 194-195, 198
Function 196
Goal 196
Lean 194-195, 198
Map 193-194
Organizing 193
Purpose 3, 187-189
Scenario 196
Steps 197
Structure 187-188
Tests 192, 197
Theme 197
Traceability 198

User Stories Applied (book) 205
User Story Mapping (book) 205

V

Version control 196
Vision document 9-26
   Analyzing problems 14-17
   Audiences 23
   Budget 3
   Contents 23-25
   Core elements of 25
   Database to track 26
   Defined 2
   Defining product 3, 9, 22
   Defining scope 21
   Defining stakeholders 23
   Identifying features 18-20
   Identifying stakeholder needs 10-13, 23
   Optional elements of 25
   Positioning the product 22, 23
   Purpose 23

W

West Broadway Gallery 206
Workflow 108-111

Writer's role
    Clarifying disagreements 6, 28
    Communicating beyond the team 6-7
    Interviewing 7
    Recording agreements 7
    Speaking up for users 6, 7
    Supporting developers 6, 7
    Writing for two audiences 1, 6, 7

Writing Effective Use Cases (book) 205

X

Y

  Yale 206

Z

Printed in Great Britain
by Amazon